T0304940

Anna Beecher is a writer from Derbyshire and London. *Here Comes the Miracle*, her first novel, was nominated for the *Sunday Times* Charlotte Aitkin Trust Young Writer of the Year Award. She performs as an oral storyteller and has written widely for theatre. Anna is a graduate of the fiction MFA at the University of Virginia. A teacher of creative writing, she divides her life between the US and UK. Her work is about love.

Also by Anna Beecher

Here Comes the Miracle

We All Come Home Alive

ANNA BEECHER

WEIDENFELD & NICOLSON

First published in Great Britain in 2025 by Weidenfeld & Nicolson,
an imprint of The Orion Publishing Group Ltd
Carmelite House, 50 Victoria Embankment
London EC4Y 0DZ

An Hachette UK Company

The authorised representative in the EEA is Hachette Ireland,
8 Castlecourt Centre, Castleknock Road, Castleknock, Dublin 15,
D15 XTP3, Republic of Ireland (email: info@hbgi.ie)

1 3 5 7 9 10 8 6 4 2

A CIP catalogue record for this book is
available from the British Library.

ISBN (Hardback) 978 1 3996 0806 0
ISBN (Ebook) 978 1 3996 0809 1
ISBN (Audio) 978 1 3996 0810 7

Typeset by Input Data Services Ltd, Bridgwater, Somerset

Printed in Great Britain by Clays Ltd, Elcograf, S.p.A.

MIX
Paper | Supporting
responsible forestry
FSC
www.fsc.org   FSC® C104740

www.weidenfeldandnicolson.co.uk
www.orionbooks.co.uk

Contents

Listen in the Dark   1

Part 1: Shock

Varieties of Shock   9

Axe Edge   23

River Thames   38

Telling   56

Smashed   71

Part 2: Holler

Apocalypse   91

Holler   106

Where Lost Things Go   121

Part 3: Home

How to Live Without Your Brother   147

At Home   168

And   198

Works Quoted   207
Acknowledgements   209

Listen in the Dark

I once asked, *What is the worst thing that's ever happened in your life?*

I was thirteen, sitting up in the dark with two other girls, my back against the textured wallpaper of the room we were sharing. It now seems like a precisely thirteen-year-old thing to say, sweet and cruel, a corollary to all that superlative talk of *favourite* colours and *best* friends, which occupies the earlier portion of childhood. A question probing for the edge of things while assuming it will encounter nothing too awful, nothing beyond the realm of the sayable.

It was my last night with these girls. We had spent two weeks together on a residential theatre course, from which I now recall only a single exercise: attempting to wriggle my hand while holding the rest of my body completely still. My interactions with the other attendees are what stay with me, the hunger with which we investigated and provoked one another. We had come from all over the country and sensed knowledge to be gleaned here that was not available at home. One evening, a languidly beautiful girl a year older than me leant against our doorframe and said, *I mean, I don't look good naked, but who does?* and I quietly pondered her question from my narrow bed. I kissed a boy whose last name rhymed with *buttock* in a game of spin the bottle and was annoyed at him for grinning afterwards; I had wanted us to seem aloof after being labelled *the most innocent people here.* I did not know then how few of my kisses would be accompanied by such unabashed happiness. And I remember this conversation in the dark. Its intimacy and urgency, the way it sprawled into the night, our time together for passing around gems of our lives running out.

A girl I will call Bella was the last to take her turn. She hesitated. The pool of empty carpet between our three beds expanded for a second in the silence.

Then she said, *My best friend died.*

For a second, I wondered if she was pretending, whether the next thing expected of me would be a laugh or some kind of playing along, as if it were a dramatic scene we were trying out. But she went on. There had been an accident in a foreign country; I pictured her friend lying in a road softened by sun. Bella said that when she was told she had repeatedly thrown up.

We stayed up together talking for a long time that night and I felt very close to both those girls, though I do not know either of them now.

*

As adults we only ask about *worst things* by accident.

At twenty-two, I found myself in a single bed, chatting with relative strangers in a dormitory at a theatre course, once again. By then, I had abandoned the idea of myself as an actor who might, say, play Lady Macbeth or a tough but troubled TV detective, but I was still interested in performance. I had come to study for a week with a Polish company whose training involved a lot of guttural singing and running around together in rhythmic step to the point of delirious exhaustion. This method worked on me just once and for a few brief minutes I felt hot and shivery and full of unselfconscious power, as if possessed, but I generally lacked the required coordination and when the other participants threw sticks at me, I just cried. There were four of us in the little dorm, talking our way towards sleep. Someone asked how many siblings everyone had, and a young woman left a small silence before her number.

You didn't sound sure about that, I laughed.

She paused again before telling us that she'd had another brother, but he had died.

The conversation lasted only a few more moments, in which I may have said, *I can't imagine that.*

I would like to go back and tell her that now I can imagine it. Now, I understand her pause in the dark.

I am no longer interested in *worst things*, which is to say, I have long outgrown the belief that experience can be organised on such neatly vertical terms. But I still want to listen in the dark, as I did in those two bedrooms a decade apart. I am interested in the pause before a revelation, that intake of breath a gap to house a ghost in.

I want to listen in the dark.

And to pull things through into the realm of the sayable. To drop into the silences between one type of reality and another. The places where life shocks us and we must come back different, if we are to return at all.

Part 1

—

Shock

Shock

(noun) *A sudden jolt or onset of emotion*
(verb) *To come into violent contact, to collide*
(verb) *To go, pass, move, journey, flee* (archaic; variant of *Shake*)

Varieties of Shock

The blow sent us skidding forward, wheels screaming over the asphalt. A silver car flew into view from behind, spinning through the air and landing on its back in the middle of the highway. All its windows shattered. Every airbag inflated.

I sat with Katie in silence, looking at it, me in the passenger seat, her in the driver's. It seemed likely that the people in the other car were dead.

An awful calm settled over me. I was calmer perhaps than I had ever been in my life, though something was leaping strangely in my chest – not my heart, but something under it.

It's OK, I said.

Katie yelled, *It's not OK*.

In that moment, either one of us might have been right.

I had been in America seven months, and Katie was my best friend there. Both of us were transplants from big cities – me from London and Katie from New York – to Charlottesville, the town in Virginia where we were attending graduate school. Two nights before, as she drove us from that town to Washington DC, we had joked that we were escaping, our laugher dashed with mania, like two teenagers slipping through the school fence together, ready to run whooping down the hill, eyes gleaming and hands clasped.

And we were borrowing back a little adolescence that weekend. On the first night we'd gone to a suburban basketball stadium to see Colombian pop sensation Maluma, taking our places at the back of a crowd made up overwhelmingly of teenage girls. We had bought cheap T-shirts and ironed photographs of Maluma onto them, his head shaved, one groomed eyebrow raised like a come-on and an elegant cut on his lip. When he walked onstage in his shining red suit, like everyone around us, we screamed.

Or at least we gave it a go. My body no longer seemed to contain the type of scream that had burst out of me aged eleven when I'd seen Boyzone at Manchester's MEN Arena, that pure high expulsion from the lungs, a torrent of want.

I was twenty-nine. When I'd first arrived in this country, where people misunderstood what I was saying surprisingly often, someone beautiful had leant over in a coffee shop and asked, *Where are you from?* in an accent similar to my own. With spectacular lack of imagination, I fell in love with the first English man I met in America. But just before this trip to Washington I had stood at the window of my janky apartment, in which nothing worked and I had to use the blue plastic cap of a milk bottle to plug the bath, watching him walk permanently away from me through the parking lot. I'd thought not, *I'll miss you*, but, *Who am I going to have a baby with?* And now here I was, still rattled, thankful to have Katie at my side, singing along to Maluma, though I don't speak Spanish and the only lyric in his entire catalogue I felt sure of was *el boom boom*.

Maluma punctuated his songs with whispers of *Maluma, baby* and his self-appointed title: *Pretty Boy Dirty Boy*. At one point he invited a girl from the crowd to join him onstage and sang her a love song. She was surprisingly placid, sitting on a high stool as he moved around her, her straightened hair a waterfall down her back. But her eyes revealed that she was not an audience plant. Her gaze widened and darted whenever he moved away to sing to the crowd, and I could feel her shock, the pounding of her heart inside her dress.

The next day we joined another crowd. The monumental March for Our Lives had been organised in the wake of the fatal shooting of fourteen students, a teacher and two staff members at Marjory Stoneman Douglas High School in Parkland, Florida. We found a spot on Pennsylvania Avenue, the broad diagonal street which links Congress and the Whitehouse, slightly contrite about the fact that it was the concert, not the protest, which had brought us to the city. Under the clear March sky, child after child came up onto the stage to describe the violence they had experienced. A boy too short for the microphone spoke of seeing his cousin shot on the way to school. The day was like a funeral. We listened to stories like his for hours, the supply of children to tell them seemingly inexhaustible.

When the eighteen-year-old Sam Fuentes came to the mic, she began, *Hello, beautiful people of America*, with a big smile. I felt dazzled, as I had before, by the confidence of Americans, the in-built ease they seemed to have with being public. Her figure on the stage was tiny from where we were, but her face was magnified on the screen behind, revealing the softness of her jaw, her young features not yet solidified, the golden glint of her small hoop earrings. A breeze moved through her hair, dyed a subtle red over her natural brown: a colour I had applied myself as a teenager, leaning over the sink, staining a towel and the rims of my ears. Six weeks before, shrapnel had travelled through Fuentes's face, irremovably lodging in her cheek and behind her eye.

She and the other Parkland students had been accused of being 'crisis actors' by conspiracy theorists. Later, when I watched her speech again on YouTube, I was struck by how difficult, perhaps impossible, it would be to fake her performance, the subtleties bubbling through it. The tiny intake of breath that threw her rhythm just slightly when she said, *It's a great day to be here and to see all of you here*, as if momentarily confused by the similarity of the two lines. The way she giggled, *Oh my God*, as she unfolded her speech, the sound coming up out of her like a leak sprung within.

As she began to read, there was a growl in her voice, under the composed pacing and lifted gaze, which might have been the earnest products of a high-school public-speaking class. She panted slightly between lines, her cheeks puffing for a second, swelling her sweet, ordinary face with its single freckle to the side of her nose, the face of a girl one might know, might have sat next to in a classroom. There was a silence and she vanished behind the podium. We did not know what was happening. Someone near me and Katie yelled, *We love you*, and others followed, and for a split second it could have been a pop concert. Fuentes emerged and almost screamed, *I just threw up on national television and it feels great.* Everyone cheered.

One of our professors had recently relayed to us the advised procedure for an active shooter on campus: turn off the lights, close the classroom door, hide under the tables pretending not to be there. We raised our eyebrows at these flimsy protections. It seemed absurd to be imagining this scenario, and yet, thirty-two people at our neighbouring university, Virginia Tech, had been killed in a shooting in 2007. Growing up in England, a single shooting entered my consciousness; it had flooded the news, our teachers had talked to us about it in solemn voices, and the children of Dunblane stood in rows on *Top of the Pops* in printed T-shirts, singing 'Knocking on Heaven's Door' and swaying with their arms at their sides. When Parkland happened, I had expected to find my classmates hugging one another in the graduate lounge or struck silent. But even though they were sad and outraged, their reactions appeared to bypass their bodies. They mentioned it briefly, then got on with things.

That night Katie and I went to a nightclub. Whiplash after the solemn day. We drank vodka and cokes and danced with men we didn't know. As the lights swirled across our faces and the sticky floor, I willed myself to keep moving, to be excited by all the open space in my life and by the people shuffling into it, slopping drinks on my shoes.

I had once attempted to swim in the Atlantic in high, ferocious waves but had swiftly been spat back onto the shore, my body scraping up the beach as the sea rejected me, leaving tiny sand cuts on my chest. Now I was in this club, abruptly single, dancing around to music I didn't like and retreating to the courtyard outside, the smoke of strangers' cigarettes drifting across my face. I left early, with enough energy to wipe off my make-up before falling asleep, and the next day, we started for home.

Our lives are punctured by moments of impossibility when the future unlatches from the present and a gap opens, which we must find a way to step over. We freeze. Our bones stiffen and we become more mineral. The world is far too bright. Sometimes that moment of impossibility stretches, and a whole season feels suspended, unreal. Sometimes it lasts just as long as it takes to sit in a car after a terrible accident, bones ringing as if struck by a tuning fork, mind ringing, wondering if those inside the vehicle that had hit us, and now lay smashed on its back in the middle of the highway, were dead.

I have two memories, which cannot both be correct.

In one I slowly tell Katie, *I am going to get out and see what happened.* I undo my seatbelt and open the door and walk along the concrete over little pieces of broken glass, to where some other cars have stopped and people are huddled, talking, the vehicles on the other side of the median speeding off to wherever they are headed. In this memory someone asks me, *Were you driving?* I answer, *No, my friend.* I find out what is going on, return to Katie and explain it to her.

In the other memory we sit still in the car for a long time, not moving or speaking. And then a man somehow emerges from the upside-down car. He is wearing a royal-blue tracksuit and stands, his clothes shining and body unscratched, in the middle of the road like a god.

No one was dead. No one was even cut. Katie came out of her car shaking and a policeman in a beige uniform appeared and spoke to us. Another man swept up the glass. We were sent to sit in the cab of the tow-truck that had arrived for Katie's car. The dim, masculine space was warm and enclosed. I felt a stillness, though that little leaping was still going beneath my ribs; I wondered if its location was my diaphragm. Whatever it was, it seemed to contain all of my panic. Katie's breath was ragged. I did not tremble, but when the policeman came to tell us that the accident had not been Katie's fault, I briefly wept, *It's not your fault, it's not your fault*, as I hugged her.

And then we were riding off and lightly flirting with the tow-truck guy, who took us to the nearest train station, Katie's wrecked car wobbling along behind us. At the drop-off point for the suburban metro stop, we found it hysterical – truly – that the area was called *Kiss and Ride*. We went shuttling back into the centre of DC, through cavernous station halls, which looked like another era's version of the future. Again, we burst into breathless laughter and couldn't stop for several minutes. It was only when we reached Union Station, where we could catch a train back to Charlottesville, and sat down in Pret a Manger to eat sandwiches which tasted of London, that Katie began to convulse and throw up black bile into her paper cup.

I laid a hand on her shoulder and said, *I'm going to call an ambulance.*

She cried, *No!* stricken with panic. *No, please don't!*

And this was the part of the day that shocked me the most.

I knew that a friend of ours was still paying off an ambulance ride at twenty-four that she'd needed at seventeen, and that another had burnt through several layers of skin on his hand and treated it at home because he doubted his insurance would cover it. But it was this moment that taught me, with the efficiency of a slap, what it means to live in America, which is to live within the boundaries of commercialised medicine. You can never completely hand yourself over to care. A little part of your brain must be awake and making calculations, even as you convulse and vomit in a public place. She laid her head on the tabletop, and I went to the counter for more napkins and cups, apologising to the people around us. And then she vomited again, and it was white and almost clear like skimmed milk. The station was draughty and there were sparrows in the rafters. Katie's back vibrated under my hands. A frown of utter confusion settled over my friend's face, but she was lucid enough to agree to going to hospital in an Uber.

The hospital was dirty. In the lobby Katie stated her name and date of birth to a receptionist. She was taken into a back room and I wasn't allowed to follow. Goldfish with ghostly frayed tails bobbed in a filthy tank; no one here was thinking of the health of the fish. Alone, I was suddenly immeasurably tired. The air conditioning was on too high, and I didn't want to remove my coat.

The impact: that great force from the back corner of the car, the way its blunt push forward also felt like a stop, as if my blood ceased pulsing as we skidded away.

My best friend in this strange country lay on the other side of a swinging hospital door. Someone must be looking at her brain. I pictured a beetroot bloodstain across it. Eventually, I was led back into the little emergency ward.

Katie's doctor told me she had a concussion, before sending me through the curtains of her cubicle to sit with her. She said hello and then immediately fell asleep.

The quality of waiting with someone in hospital is different to waiting anywhere else. I remembered being beside my brother's sickbed in Oxford – John, his body and gown and bedsheet so thin – sitting there with my coffee cup and red jumper and good health; the protective clothing of the outside world; the guilt and relief when I got up to go. I watched Katie sleeping and drew her in my notebook – a picture I could never show her because she looked like a corpse. She was woken and taken away for a test. I sat on the chair in her empty cubicle and listened to a man yelling, *Hello, hello?* I heard a doctor arrive and begin to ask quiet questions. The man asked loudly, *How much sodium is in a boiled egg?* and the doctor replied, *I don't know off the top of my head how much sodium is in a boiled egg.* His voice was weary. It was clearly not the issue at hand.

Overleaf from my sketch of Katie is a dictionary entry I had transcribed just days before:

> **Blindside**: *Verb: North American. Hit or attack (someone) on the blindside. Catch (someone) unprepared; attack from an unexpected position.*

The urge to tell the English Man that I loved him had been growing in me for a month. The three words played on a loop in my mind, though the thought of releasing them made me feel like throwing up, which seemed in hindsight like a bad sign. At last, a week ago, I'd said it. We were lying together in my bed. And I knew, in the silence which followed, that this man was falling away from me, even though for six months he had been so kind. Eventually, he'd whispered, *I'm not ready to say that yet.* I lay next to him, between us my torrent of want. *What are you waiting for?* I thought. *What else could you need to know?*

So began my spate of transcriptions from the dictionary, my handwriting neater than usual, as if to shore up the clarifying magic of the definitions of words. I wrote out: **Love**: *a strong feeling of affection and sexual attraction for someone*, and read it aloud to him, to check that our issue was not semantic. Then off he went forever in his long grey coat, down the wooden fire escape, where I had recently seen my first raccoon – my brain glitching at the unfamiliarity of the animal, stuttering up the word *cat, cat*, while I slowly worked out what it actually was.

The break-up had come with so little warning. My friends seemed to share my disbelief; Katie and another friend came over within half an hour and we laughed a lot on my cheap, uncomfortable sofa. Jangly with the suddenness of it, I kept repeating, *I'm OK, I'm OK*, but there was a weird sensation in my chest.

Later I discovered that break-ups and other shocks can cause an excess of cortisol, which sends blood to the major muscles. The foolish muscles tense, ready to fight or flee, but there's nothing to be done, and so the blood sits there making the body feel too tight for all it contains, like there's a fist around the heart.

When we came out of the hospital I couldn't stop saying, *We've been in a car accident.*

I told the Uber driver and the receptionist in the hotel we went to, paid for by Katie's parents. It was gleamingly clean, and I imagined the most expensive place I'd ever stayed. *Thank you, we have been in a car accident,* I said to the porter who carried our bags to our room, and, *Sorry, I have been in a car accident,* to the women in the café next door, in explanation of my slowness, my inability to make choices. Eventually I bought soup, which I placed by Katie's bed, though of course she didn't touch it.

That night I sat at the hotel bar as she slept on upstairs, my mind returning and returning to the impact. It was quiet. The booths glowed softly and the chrome rail along the bar's edge shone. *I have been in a car accident,* I said to the Irish barman and to the big guy beside me who told me he was in town for a conference and that he'd had six concussions due to playing football in college. My martini was briny and cold, and both men tried to pay for it: the perks of being a woman alone.

What if I abdicated from love? I wondered. But love has always just come for me, crashed into me with a kind of unstoppable violence.

*

We say things are *put* into perspective, but the word *put* feels far too careful, too much like *placed*, when things so often *crash* into perspective, unlikely events colliding with great force. I call this week, half joking, *the most eventful week of my life*. The next day, I sold my first novel to a publisher. I talked to the editor on the phone from London, her voice full of excitement, as a friend who happened to also be visiting DC ferried Katie and I home in his car. After sending my draft out for publishers to consider, I had felt the want flowing from me as I walked through my days, shimmering and diffusing where my body's edges met the air. Now here was all that want being met. The phone call was wonderful, my concussed friend drifting in and out of sleep beside me on the backseat, my neck rigid. The editor and I spoke for a long stretch of highway, and I stiffened when other cars drew too close, the remembered impact jolting again and again through my mind and my spine.

A year after the accident, Katie lent me her copy of the short-story collection *Jesus' Son* by Denis Johnson. I read 'Car Crash While Hitchhiking', on which her wonderful younger self had written comments like, *Wow*, and, *Oh my fucking God*, in the margins. The deadbeat protagonist lists the drivers who have picked him up, ending with 'a family from Marshalltown who head-onned and killed forever a man driving West out of Bethany Missouri'. It was the redundant *forever* in the line that flipped something below my ribs for a second: my heart or my diaphragm.

By this time, my mind had almost stopped its habitual returns to the moment of impact, the burning screeching sound, and the moment after, the sweeping of glass. But I knew that a parallel reality existed where the man in the silver car had died. Where the car had contained not only him, but children, a whole family. And sometimes I thought about how Katie and I would have carried that, returning to our classes with a stranger's death inside us, never able to undo or unshare it. How it would have held us both together and apart.

But that is not what became of us. In this story, we all come home alive.

Axe Edge

I was fifteen. Over my detested school uniform, I wore a ketchup-red coat: a chosen danger at a school where boldness never went unpunished.

The morning began as they all did. I walked the straight line from my home to the marketplace, a sheet of grey tarmac beneath a sheet of grey sky. I crossed it and continued down the steep hill of Bath Road. I'd beaten this path each weekday for four years, so my body navigated, leaving my brain to skitter through tactics for surviving the day. At the bottom of the hill, I always turned left down a road of tall sycamores, before finally passing through steel railings onto school property.

Except this day, I did not. I turned right instead and walked away from school, feeling the place recede behind me.

Impossible is an absolute word. 'More impossible' is incorrect in the same way as 'very unique'. And yet, school – turning up and hearing my name called and my mortifying voice answer, *Yes Miss*, moving through each day with whispers touching my skin – had begun to feel more and more impossible.

A girl who I will call Poppy had been my closest friend for a while, and then, with little warning, she wasn't my friend at all, then more girls weren't, then the boys tagged mutely behind them, then at last everyone seemed to be talking about me but no one was allowed to talk to me.

Poppy and I had had the kind of entwined friendship that manifests in younger children as the sharing of headlice and in teenage girls as the sharing of secrets. She washed her dark hair then blow-dried and straightened it every single night. She could do an eyeliner cat flick and used thick, viscous mascara that made her lashes look like spider-legs. Our mothers were friends and for a time all four of us were united in the Atkins diet, adding melted cheese to our fried eggs. We shared an interest in our own bodies, the ways we could intervene in their presentation and shape, the ways we might use them in the world. Poppy and I spent long afternoons lying on her bed trying to tan through the window in the weak Derby-shire sunlight, not realising the right kind of rays couldn't touch us through the glass. In school we had learnt about earthquakes and the founding of the National Health Service, so we called our recollections of how many cans of beer or bottles of cheap warm wine or vodka we had drunk in a night *The Beveridge Report*, and our assessment of which girls had gone furthest sexually *The Richter Scale*.

With Poppy, I felt mirthful and rebellious. We laughed at the back of our classes until we couldn't breathe.

I knew about the brutality of children. At eleven, a blonde girl with a pointed face had yanked out a handful of my hair. At twelve, a group had chased me as I walked home, encircled me and spat on me. These incidents were put down to my *weird clothes*, though I now see my bright colours as armour; by giving them external things to ridicule, I could assuage my fear that something more fundamental about me had been sniffed out, something *off*. And there was a sort of camaraderie in it. All the kids at my school in the wrong coats and trainers bunched together at breaktimes, sharing outrage when rocks sailed over the bush towards us. The day one struck a boy on the temple and blood gushed out, matting into his hair, we relished the drama.

When I fell out with Poppy, adults consoled me with variations on *girls are vicious*, noting with a sort of approval that boys hit and got it over with. But I *had* been hit by girls when younger; it was a girl who had pulled out my hair, a girl who tugged a chair from behind me as I went to sit, my coccyx and my dropped apple smashing against the ground. It wasn't until our middle teens that the bullying lost its frank physicality.

Our violence changed as our bodies did.

Most girls have a moment as they enter their adolescence, or earlier, when the world announces, *Your body is not your own.* Mine was in a car park in Stockport. It was the middle of the afternoon. My mum and I stopped to ask for directions and a man moved up behind me on the concrete and placed his hand on my twelve-year-old buttock while his associate told her the lefts and rights. At the time I thought, *That was weird,* as though a glitch had occurred in reality and things would now return to normal. But you can only feel this way once. The accrual of such moments teaches you that they are not anomalies, these touches and stares and jokes. So you turn this attention, which feels like danger, into power. Heels, a low top and a push-up bra can grant access to the land of the grown-ups. You can sit in the pub at fourteen shredding damp beer mats and drinking a vodka and orange, as if you are in charge of your life. You can let a bouncer take in your body and meet his eye as if to say, *ID me and you've just given that look to a child,* then walk past him into the narrow, box-like nightclub that smells of sweet sharp shots and Lynx Africa over sweat. It was a leverage deployed indirectly, more like magic than strength. Of course, girls bully with cunning. And, of course, our fallouts so often centre on how this power is being used, who is being too sexual and who not enough. We were obsessed with each other's choices because we needed to believe that our own would matter, that they would determine what became of us.

My problem with Poppy stemmed from my body: things I did and things done to me after we'd burnt our throats with vodka; my fourteen-year-old mouth as I knelt in a bank of grass; my fifteen-year-old back on a bare mattress on the floor in a room above a bar; my menstrual blood flowing down a boy's thin forearm in the dim light of a caravan; my skin against the milk-white skin of another girl. There were many rules. Hand jobs meant you weren't frigid, but blow jobs made you a slut. If you did something with a boy, your behaviour alone would be judged, almost as if he had not also been there. If you did something with a girl, it must be sanitised watermelon-lip-gloss-kissing in front of boys, nothing below the neck, never, ever a pulse of real desire. It was as if these rules had all been decided on a day when I wasn't there; I only seemed to discover them upon breaking them. And my body was always breaking them.

The problem stemmed from Poppy's body as well. When we were still in the stage of our friendship that was all confessions, she would talk about how hard she found that body to live in, calling the issue, *My Shape.* At school, on a Personal Social Health Education Day, we sat on the floor in a windowless classroom, instructed to list our good qualities inside a photocopied outline of a person. Noticing that Poppy had written nothing, the teaching assistant offered, *Pretty?* to get her started. As if it were a neutral suggestion. Poppy laughed, then stared blankly at the page through her spider-leg lashes, tears welling in her eyes without falling, refusing to write a single word. A danger crackled through our lives at this time, a dark sense that *pretty* really might be the soil in which all our other merits must be planted. Where did that leave us if we didn't have it or if we had the wrong sort? The problems between us stemmed from our having female bodies at all.

And all of my memories of my body at this age are wrong. I looked at photographs when I began to write this, thinking that I needed to recall the dimensions of the school corridors, the nicotine-teeth shade of the tiles in the science rooms. But I have retained those details precisely. What surprised me were my own dimensions, and Poppy's. Though my body occasionally seemed to me, if not truly attractive, then useful – when momentarily charged by another person's desire – I also imagined it to be wrong in some conspicuous way, and too big. But in all the photos, and in a video of me dancing alone across the scuffed floor of the empty school hall, I was shocked to see that my body was simply ordinary. Nothing to lament or correct. In one image, Poppy and I sit in a cluster of girls, five of us gathered on a metal bench. I am in the centre, my hands and shoulders raised in a smiling shrug. Poppy is laughing beside me, all of us crushed in close. I am a little larger than the skinniest – a girl with very long hair who looks like a beautiful newt – and Poppy is a little larger than me. I long to climb into that photograph and tell us, *Girls, you are fine, you are lovely, you were so recently little children.*

There are so many ways in which you can get having a body wrong at fifteen. It is a paltry space in which to live.

Sometimes we had to shove one another out, to make a little room for ourselves.

And I shoved Poppy, at least once. At a party in another kid's living room, she pointedly implied I was a slut for drunkenly running along the dark street in my bra, so I pointedly noted to a group of boys, who were discussing the relative merits and demerits of various female body parts, that girls with big boobs usually had fat bottoms, *so it's a trade-off*. Here: a sharp, true shard of the parallel story in which I was the bitch.

If the campaign against me was about my body, it was also about the opposite of my body, some abstract sense of me in virtual space, which I could not touch or conceal.

It was 2003 and something happened that none of the adults in our lives could imagine and we could barely imagine ourselves. A fake profile, seeming to be mine, appeared on the internet. The voice of this profile said horrible things about Poppy on the comment thread of someone's personal Freewebs site, the customisable platform we all used before any of us had heard of Facebook. The profile had the mean thoughts of someone who should rightfully be hated.

At first all I knew was that there had been a shift; the anger of my former friends had spread, without warning, to everyone. I came into a classroom and discovered that no other pupil would look at me, their unanimity a wall.

When I at last pieced together what was going on, I felt a bleak helplessness. It was the peak of the mounting impossibility; proving that it was not me who had typed nasty things onto the purple wall of that Freewebs site was like proving an object not to exist. I began walking around and around the school every breaktime, so as not to provide a static target for globs of wet toilet paper thrown at the back of my neck. I avoided the areas where one could be watched from above. I skipped lunch so that no one would see me sitting alone, and at the end of the day I hid in the toilets, waiting for the quiet that signalled I could walk home in peace.

Writing this now, from the distance of sixteen years and another continent, an old shiver of mortification travels over my skin – not at having been an outcast, but at caring; having cared then and caring enough now to write this. Still, my care feels like a mark against me, evidence that I deserved it. *Don't let it get to you*, is the cardinal rule of school. But I did. I remember a teacher shouting, *This teenage angst doesn't wash with me*, when I drew or maybe compass-scratched some cliché into a desk, a skull perhaps, and was noticed to have scabbed tracks emerging from the cuffs of my school shirt after slashing my skin with an orange disposable razor. But if he was right that there was a degree of performance to my actions, he was wrong to imagine it was for him. Children are told repeatedly, *Tell an adult if you are being bullied*, but they quickly intuit that it won't work. We feel the insult in the implication that a word from them might undo our dramas, which we are so invested in. Besides, we do not want their justice, decrees from above to *all just get along.* Only our own justice – readmittance to the group or, even better, the swapping of alliances – can absolve us. We know adults can never puncture the membrane and intervene in our world.

When you are in school, it fills your entire remembered life. I don't know now how long I was a pariah. Perhaps it felt longer than it really was because I could see no prospect of it ending. I couldn't picture a future beyond carpets spotted black with trodden-down gum, the scrape of chair legs on tile, safety glass and strip lights, pink salt gritting the icy playground and radiators that wouldn't turn off in summer, the peeling Fleetwood Mac display in the music corridor, the sting of an AstroTurf graze. We were forever learning about the history of woollen mills and attempting to augment our sexless uniforms, ever envious of the girl in the year above whose white shirt had a tiny black heart stitched onto a little tag above the hem. I would lie in bed at night, wondering how I was going to get through another day. I sensed danger, from my former friends, but most of all from my own shame.

Then the morning came when my body simply refused to go.

Walking away from school immediately felt correct. Adrenaline, a kind of focused determination I had not experienced in weeks, broke the fog of my sadness. Snow on the hills, it was the type of morning that would freeze ice crystals into wet hair. I walked down the street that edged the park, onto the next street and the next, not thinking of where I was going, gradually rising up and up as I moved further from school, until a final long road pulled me out of town completely. I was overjoyed when the pavement vanished under my black school shoes, replaced by grass patched with snow.

Before I knew it, I had arrived on Axe Edge Moor, which was covered all over in white.

The moor was an expanse between my hometown and the rest of the world, contoured by fissures and small abandoned mines. On the other side of it lay the glamour of Macclesfield, with its bowling alley and Mexican restaurant. Earth and sky could blur up there, the boundary softened by mist, and the land could also seem like water, horizontal but moving, waves of wind stirring the low-growing plants. It was a place where rivers began, fed by the rain, which gathered in the heather and gritstone. The Dove, the Manifold and the Wye flowed east to the North Sea. The Dane and the Goyt flowed west into the Mersey, then the Irish Sea and the Atlantic.

I walked on, unbuttoning my red coat, following the curve of the road. Grass and heather barbed through the white ground. More snow began to fall. A prickling cold spread over my nose and face and gloveless hands.

At some point, I started to sing – Courtney Love, patron saint of teenage girls other people's parents ban from parties. Song drew the chill air more deeply into my lungs, where it warmed briefly before releasing, visible for just a moment before it dissipated.

I walked for a few hours. There was no destination on the other side of the walking, just a sense that the walking itself, if I went far enough, would make me vanish and I would no longer have to deal with my life.

Eventually, I was spotted by two police officers, a man and woman who were driving over the moor, my red coat conspicuous against the snow. They were brisk but not unkind. I could not be left alone wandering about in that hypothermic place, ridden with bogs and holes. *You could die up here.* I was driven home, all my walking undone in twenty minutes. My dad was there, working upstairs in his pottery, clay circling under his hands, drying his palms and wearing down his wedding band. I remember standing at the door with the officers, but not the look on my father's face. He thanked them, very polite.

It was a Friday, and that evening my parents agreed that I would not go back to school on Monday. And, in fact, except for one brief meeting with the headmaster to formalise my exit, I never went back again.

I had not vanished on the moor, but the walking had done something, even if only in persuading the adults around me that I had reached an unsustainable level of recklessness.

I knew little about the moor on that day when I walked out onto it. Instinct kept me near the road, but I don't think I had a concrete sense of danger, of the loose rocks covered by snow and abandoned mineshafts. I also did not know that the rock under my feet was 300 million years old, and the coiling ferns beneath the snow just as ancient, the remains of a world that had lizards and frogs but no people. Back then, I had never thought to wonder where the rivers in my life began. I had seen friends drunkenly vomit into the Wye, their bellies pressing into the limestone side of a bridge, and a few times a year its water ran orange through the park, the shade of tinned tomato soup, because of iron deposits left over from the mines. I had often waded into that river in jelly shoes with a group of other children, our mothers on a picnic blanket on the bank, drinking wine. There were only women and children on those bright afternoons, and later, when one of the other mothers died, I would remember the River Wye and the park beside it as a sort of church – a space that waited for us to enter it in community. I used to crouch in the River Goyt with my father building sculptures from stones, little towers of rock, and once a crocodile. And it was to the Goyt Valley that he went with Poppy's mum after I left school. They released their dogs into the grass and tried to negotiate on our behalf. I knew afterwards that he had stood up for me. I also knew that she had told him some of the most lacerating gossip about me: I had had sex with another girl at a party. When he reported the conversation back to me, his voice was different, and this detail was a tiny rip in the story where the bullying wasn't my fault.

I heard you ran away, then ran back, everyone said.

And it is true that nothing really happened to me up on the moor, except a little snow landing and melting in my hair. Even the location is not as melodramatic as it sounds; three of the four roads out of that town rise up into moorland.

But the moor is powerful.

Maybe I did briefly pass into the white space of not being up there, between the wet ground and the sky.

Or perhaps it was the opposite: an absolute kind of being. For when there is no space for you – when you are mandated to put on a uniform and go to a building each day where you feel ashamed and afraid – it is astonishing to walk alone out in the open, seen only by things that cannot judge you.

Where I turned right instead of left, the place on the pavement where my feet refused to carry me to that school: this is the point I have continued to walk away from. I have never been suicidal. I used to wonder if I had, but when that dark urge took hold of a friend, the animal of it uncoiling under his skin, making his green eyes both intense and vacant, I knew I was meeting a force unknown to me. But I have wanted not to be. And in all those moments, I have moved. Taken my body elsewhere.

*

Back when school stretched across my remembered life, I worried the bullying would always live close to my surface and I would become a bitter, flinching adult, reluctant to risk friendship at all. But, in fact, the experience came into my body and left it again – air into song into air – because of the friends I made afterwards. I saw out my GCSEs quietly at a new school and then moved to London, having idly googled *free performing arts school* one day in the IT room and discovering to my amazement that one existed. On my second day at that new school, a group of terrifyingly confident students asked if I wanted to go to Tesco for lunch and I went, nervously, looking for the trick in it. Weeks passed without a wet glob of toilet paper hitting my neck or hearing my name whispered in the halls and I thought less and less about where to put my hands. Then a girl and a boy called for me at home, with a bunch of yellow chrysanthemums wrapped in clear cellophane, and I let them in. I still see them on my threshold, Rachel's short hair and flowers in Danny's arms, the sky behind them a London September blue. They'll never know what they did for me, those friends. Their kindness loosened the fear clenched in my body. They are among the loves of my life.

My life has shocked me. One of the shocks has been sadness, but the greater shock has been joy. That unforeseen opening of space. I feel the hard flint of joy within my chest, the strength of it. It has stunned me with its refusal to be repressed.

And so, I think not of walking away but towards. For I have kept walking out and out onto Axe Edge Moor, the urge ever returning to stride into somewhere bigger, wilder, more dangerous and more beautiful than where I stand.

River Thames

I had two brothers, Max and John. They were identical twins two years older than me, part of the architecture of my life from the moment I was born. As a child I couldn't comprehend how others couldn't tell them apart. It is only in adulthood, looking through the old photograph albums our mum will no longer open, that I've experienced the thought, *Is that Max or John?* In life they were always distinct, their like features put to different uses. Max – a born performer who pierced the ears of all our teenage friends and grew up to be a contortionist, to go by *they* and wear bright blooms of eyeshadow above a thick beard. John – a curator of things, postcards and pencils placed in exact positions on his desk, whose boyhood quietness intensified into a small white flame of thought. John grew up into a history student who wrote things down in small black letters in small black notebooks and died.

John started a PhD at Oxford at twenty-four. Max and I took the piss out of him for being part of that rarified world, from which he visited with the fresh knowledge that cheese should be cut using a special knife with a curved, forked tip. But we were proud of him. He'd been there just briefly when his cancer was discovered. This was followed by a single almost-year in which so much fell away from him and from all three of us, including our blithe feeling of immortality and his life of study, which he had to leave for the kingdom of the sick. His final weeks brought a rapid succession of endings: the end of leaving the house, of leaving the hospital, of leaving bed, the end of eating, talking, waking and finally pain, which slipped away as he did. It was mid-December. In the bewildered intimacy of new grief, I lay on the sofa with Max, our bodies pressed close for survival, like beings just born.

That almost-year had shrunk our parents. They were thin with worry, our mother's consuming denial and our father's pragmatism both a kind of pre-emptive grief. Before all four of us (and how strange it was to no longer be five) stretched a future we could not imagine.

Mercifully, a series of tasks emerged for us to complete.

A woman in a grey pencil skirt and pumps appeared at the hospice and spread a catalogue of coffins before us. When we said *simple*, she assumed we were politely saying *cheap*, and turned pages showing coffins decorated with dolphins and footballs. My family had always laughed a lot and our laughter came then and sat beside us in the room, John's body still close, just on the other side of the door. Max led the way in selecting the coffin, having apparently discussed John's preferences with him in a cocktail bar a few months before.

A place and date needed to be chosen for his burial. We picked Wolvercote Cemetery in Oxford. It had never occurred to me that burial slots could be fully booked like hair appointments, but very few options were available; we had to go with Christmas Eve or leave his body in cold storage a whole extra month. The rain was torrential when that day came, like an act of God.

In January we held a memorial, for which songs had to be chosen and catering arranged: 'Amazing Grace', miniature scones. In the pew of the chapel, I held an order of service over my mouth and slid my tongue in rhythmic circles over my teeth to warm up my voice, as I would for any performance. Then I stood and walked to the front and gave a speech.

The tasks thinned out.

For a year John's bedroom sat untouched, his black-rimmed glasses waiting on the desk as if he might return to claim them. Eventually my dad and I knelt on the carpet and sorted everything into piles. I printed, *From the Library of John Beecher*, into the front of his hundreds of paperbacks, with a stamp I'd had specially made. I incorporated his small impersonal items into my life as best I could, using his pens until the ink dried.

Another year passed before the last task came.

My dad picked me up in his ageing Honda and we drove to a field in the Surrey Hills to go shopping for gravestones. His eyes were dry but pink as brick dust.

Again, it was raining, this time in fine mist; my canvas shoes sunk into mud when I climbed from the car. A man with a ponytail led us between the stones. All were craggy and unpolished, like forms just found there in the grass. Letters could be added, he said, and left bare or filled in with white. Some stones had perfect circles cut through them and there was something beguiling about these neat voids, as if one might reach through them and touch a different world.

We wanted limestone because our family had lived for thirteen years in a limestone house, not far from a quarry that sent subtle judders through our hometown. Where other children had sandpits, my brothers and I had played in a pit of wet lime, stacking it, clawing gorges from it with our small hands, sluicing it smooth with plastic bucketfuls of water and coming into the house filthy, our palms grey and dried tight. The stone my dad and I decided on was nearly rectangular but with irregular edges and diagonal along the top. It was almost a classic gravestone but rougher, more loosely drawn.

What was our impulse to eschew neatness, the work of human hands, to pick something that might have sprung from the earth with my brother's name on it? A desire not to prettify his death at twenty-five, because it was obscene? Or a desire to accept it as a phenomenon of the world, like rock or river, lichen or grass? We asked for John's name to be added, the word *Beloved* – my mum's request – and the dates of his life. Then we paid for it and left.

*

The business of his death was now complete and all that remained was to remember.

On anniversaries, we did things John would have liked, exploring second-hand bookshops or dropping down onto the edge of the Thames and digging clay pipes from the mud, water-aged and white, like thin, hollow bones. We never visited the grave. John had lived and been buried in Oxford, and the rest of the family were in London, so it was easy to avoid.

But one day, by chance, we drove close. None of us mentioned the signs for Wolvercote Cemetery or the fact my mother was weeping. That unexpected proximity was a stinging shock.

I began to have doubts about the headstone. What if John's name had been misspelled, or the dates of his life were incorrect? None of us had seen it in situ. What if the man with the ponytail had taken our money and never installed it? It started to feel important to go there and check. Perhaps there was one more thing John required of me after all.

It would have taken just a few hours to reach the cemetery by public transport, but I needed longer to prepare myself for the sight of my brother's death made official, written in stone. On foot, the journey would take six days, following a snaking path along the River Thames. If I stuck to the river, it would be 150 miles from door to grave. I hoped those miles would help me pinpoint the place, inscribe its coordinates on my body, so its location could never shock me again.

It was October 2015. I was twenty-six years old and almost three years out from John's death. The night before I left, Danny, my school friend and now housemate, made a cake, with icing so thick that it hung in folds over the sponge like a tablecloth, *Good Luck Anna* written across it in blue. At its base, he had arranged a ring of halved strawberries.

The next morning, I closed the front door behind me and walked uphill, through streets of brick and net curtains to Crystal Palace. I'd expected a pilgrim's sense of calm, but, of course, as the London day began around me, my mind was full of its usual clutter. A man I'd fallen swiftly and stupidly in love with lived in Streatham, and as I passed through it, I felt a small spark of hunger just at being near his flat.

I walked on to Wimbledon, where I had worked for years as a playleader, shaking a half-moon tambourine and singing instructions as small children scrambled over ramps and slides. Once, John had come to meet me there, so that we could go for dinner at the end of my shift. He was between rounds of chemotherapy, strong and talkative, and we'd gone for burritos in a place with a corrugated metal floor. When I hear the dull command, *Live everyday as if it's your last*, I think of all the precious mundane days like that one, which I enjoyed unrushed, assuming there would be countless more ahead.

Wimbledon Common seemed like a gateway out of the city, its green softness a relief after hours of pavement. It was very quiet, with no one around but a grey heron and a scatter of smaller birds drinking from a pool in the rain. In Richmond Park the deer lifted their heads to watch me but did not startle when I approached to photograph the pale tips of their antlers. London was falling away as I passed through these animals, the river drawing close.

When the Thames at last appeared, downhill from me, framed by trees, the sight sent joy through my limbs, like that first world-expanding glimpse of the ocean on holiday. I rang the bell at the Richmond–Twickenham ferry, half expecting a silent, ancient figure with a white beard to row me across. But the ferryman was a teenager, with a single glinting earring. Because he asked, I told him my destination, and on the other side he refused to take my pound.

It was dark by the time I arrived for the night at a friend's house outside of Twickenham. Nineteen miles into my journey, my body felt ragged. I'd often walked the three hours of pavement from London's Zone 1 to Zone 4, a habit acquired in the first flush of grief, when I'd been restless and craved repetitive movement, but a whole day of walking had exhausted me. There was stiffness in my muscles that I knew would solidify as I slept, so that my first miles the next day would feel like thawing out. My friend fed me and washed my sore feet. Doubt

crossed her face when I told her how much further I had
to go.

I crept out early the next day, the streets empty and dim.
At the river, a man gestured to the rain and said, *Miserable
weather*, by way of greeting. It dawned on me that he
thought I was out for a brief stroll, that no one could tell
what I was up to.

Once, while working for a theatre company, I'd picked
up a thin, silver sword from a theatrical weapon hire and
carried it to rehearsal on the Tube in an inconspicuous
case. As my long walk went on, I began to feel like I had a
similarly unlikely object about my person. I found myself
wanting to tell a woman feeding ducks outside a riverfront
house, *I'll be walking all week! My destination is a grave!* But
I soon realised that there was something strangers could
offer me, precisely because they didn't know. *Look at that*,
a farmer said as we crossed in a field, and I glanced up and
saw a long, low rainbow. I wanted to chase after him and
thank him, because he had given it to me so lightly, not
knowing I needed it.

I can tell the journey in impressions now: swans travelling
in rings of ripples; the skinny Victorian building with
a stranger's hairs in the bath where I slept in Staines at
the end of my second day; the cage of white doves in a
riverside garden; the liquid plasters I painted over the
knuckles of my toes as the week wore on. But at the time,
each day was long, distinct and often painful. Loss is also

like this; you move through it doggedly, incrementally, and time blurs much of its sharpness.

My brain circled back to sex and the man in Streatham, the calm gloom of his bedroom as the radiator filled with water, my copper-brown dress on his floorboards, charged with static, gathering all the lint. *You make me feel bronze*, I had told him, *third place*. Now, I walked over yellow aspen leaves and tried to push him from my thoughts. But nothing more fitting replaced him, just the cast of other people I had been seeing; I had stood on a balcony above this same river just a week before, looking out over Limehouse, while a different person kissed my neck in the cold. I seemed to have emerged from the glassy first chamber of grief, hungry and shocked to find myself still young, seeking skin. The walking was not entirely separate from this. *I am alive*, both whispered, *let's see what this body can do*.

It might have helped my focus had I known more names for the things I was seeing, but I did not have *black bent* or *cocksfoot*, *couch* or *fescue* in my vocabulary then, just *grass*. *Bread and cheese* rose from my memory, delighting me, as the name of a hedge, but I did not know to also call it *hawthorn*, or that the beautiful red-brown birds that stood among the ducks were *Egyptian geese*. I entered Runnymede, where high marks stood on a wall with dates of floods – *March 1947, November 1894* – below a painted red seal and the words, *Magna Carta*. My sense of history was like my sense of nature. Isolated phrases swam into my mind, when what I wanted were whole sentences, whole paragraphs of explanation. My brother could have told me all of it, had he walked at my side. A historian, facts didn't sluice in and out of John's brain as they did through mine.

Wednesday, my third day, was one of my easiest walks, at fifteen miles, though as I write this, years later and so much softer with myself, that still seems quite far for my short, sore legs to have carried me. I came off the river for a few hours to take the Long Walk up to Windsor Castle, the manicured path so straight and solid after the water, which was steely when I returned to it, the sky above it grey. For a while the world seemed brittle, plants drying out for winter, dead thistles yellowing at the mouth of a stone bridge, grass like straw, barbed wire and brambles, an industrial yard with heaps of fine ground rock and squat dirty towers against the sky. Then suddenly a meadow of pink cosmos and orange poppies, then a field with rows and rows of cabbages, small furrows between them shining wet, everything fresh and alive again, as if occupying its own separate season. This world that no longer held my brother was so varied, even along this one short stretch of river. I felt entrusted with it, as if he had passed it to me only as he left.

Rowers were out at Maidenhead. The seagulls above them scattered as if hurled from their hands into the air. I passed through a riverside park with a memorial fountain, the water dribbling from the mouths of lions. Nearby, someone had scratched *REDBUM* into the dark moss on the wall. I walked on, my leggings damp with sweat and my lower back aching. The sight of an old railway line, grass beginning to reclaim it, made me feel inexplicably alone. Light touched the rails where they curved and vanished into the hedges.

When I reached my Airbnb in Cookham, I dropped onto the bed, before even removing my backpack. Straight away, I felt moisture underneath me, but I couldn't get up. With a sinking certainty, I knew my period had come, perhaps hours before. When I stood, the sheets were printed with a scarlet butterfly. I stripped the bed, listened for confirmation that my host was downstairs, then tiptoed across the hall to rinse my blood from the sheets, embarrassed to be seen.

I used to think of discipline and a sort of mortification as keys that I could turn to open hidden, better parts of myself, things underneath my surface, purposeful and pure. At fifteen, when I began to dance en pointe, I watched with fascination as dark spots formed under my big toenails, bruises yearning to break open and bleed. They began at the nailbed, then spread until the whole area was black. Then the nails loosened and fell off, leaving the battered skin soft, ugly and naked underneath. I wasn't at all good at ballet, but *this* was my achievement, as if my toughness might count against my lack of grace. Throughout my twenties I rose early to write before work, feeling slightly superior to those who used

4 a.m. for sleeping. I sensed that something vital might be gleaned from giving up foods for Lent. It took until I was twenty-nine for me to become suspicious of the part of myself that grows smug under punishment and I am still unlocking the rooms and long wild gardens that can open in a life when one simply rests and eats.

On Thursday morning, I set off from Cookham determined to walk twenty-six miles by nightfall. The sky was pink, light on the tips of the grass and tall, swaying bodies of the teasels. We associate the outdoors with openness, but as I made my way to the river, down a path boundaried on one side by trees and on the other a low hedge, I loved the sense of a being in a corridor, the limiting of my options to *forward* or *back*. London could be brutal, especially in my grief, with so many thousands of choices to be made within its net of streets. On the river, forward was the simplest proposition. Back would be just as hard on my body and moving ahead promised new things. And each boat along the water's edge, with a name and a few objects visible at the low windows, offered a life to my imagination. The Thames was hazy at my first sight of it that morning, behind a bank of laurel. It felt intimate to have seen so much of the river's snaking body. To meet it once more in the privacy of dawn.

By lunch, I reached Marlow, where I drifted to sleep in a café. I counted the miles left and the hours before dusk and decided to cut a corner off the next leg of my walk, taking a straight line through what looked like fields on my phone map instead of following the bend of the river. Feeling light and purposeful, I made my way out of the town, and then through a small woodland dappled with afternoon sun, a little exhilarated by breaking my own plans. I felt like I could reach Oxford easily this way, stepping from sunspot to sunspot all the way there. But at some point, after an hour or two of my clever diversion, I became lost in a network of fields and woods joined by unmade roads. At the husk of a tree where the outer bark stood hollow as if the young wood within had walked off, abandoning its coat, I sat heavily on the ground to examine my map. But there was no blue dot to tell me where I was. GPS was out of range. I scanned my surrounding for signposts: nothing. Soon the day would run out of light. I stood, trying to harness the energy of my fluttering panic, and started in a plausible direction. I had told myself, inexplicably, that squirrels were lucky, so whenever a silver streak appeared ahead of me, I was briefly bolstered. Until I came across one, lying dead on its back, the white fur of its stomach jewelled with blood.

Eventually I clambered over a stile into a field and spotted a tiny pub perched on the other side of it. I grabbed my phone from my pocket and could at last see where I was, not far after all from the hostel that was my final destination for the night – really just one long road in it. But, beneath the low ceiling of the pub, the barman laughed when I asked if it was walkable. The road I had spotted on the map was a motorway. I couldn't make it on foot. Men at a corner table laughed too, when I asked if there were other routes I might take, or somewhere close by I could sleep that night if not. And I could see that I was ridiculous to them all, so small and out of place in my muddy leggings and backpack, a girl with no idea where she was. In the car park I burst into tears, and then a blonde woman climbed out of a car I had thought to be empty. She came over to me and soon I was in her car. How quickly the world moved beneath us as she took me twenty minutes down the motorway to my bed for the night. I do not remember her name now (it may have been Kay), just that there was a lipsticked glamour about her against my dishevelled state, and her unhesitating kindness.

In the youth hostel in Streatley I slept in an empty dormitory, choosing a high bunk in the corner. Slipping out at 5 a.m., I listened to the Proclaimers in my headphones: *I would walk five hundred miles.* It was freezing, and I felt bruised, embarrassed in front of myself at getting lost the day before. But then I saw a movement as I came onto the path that would return me to my guiding companion, the Thames. A hare dashed from the hedge, paused, alertness in its whole muscular body, and looked at me. It was the first I had seen in the world. The gift of that look carried me a whole day more.

The last town I stayed in was Abingdon. As I devoured chips in a pub there, the barmaid asked, *Are you staying at Morgan's house?* My host for the night had told her that his guest was a young woman on a journey of many miles.

Finally, my exhaustion and hunger and muddy shoes had exposed my secret mission to strangers.

The next day, I re-dressed my blistered feet in plasters and stepped out one last time into the dawn. It was Saturday. As I approached Oxford a strange worry came: what if, after all this, the grave wasn't there? Anxiety caused my stomach to cramp, the pain so intense that I had to sit down in the grass beside the path. But I carried on, leaving my river behind.

Oxford opened around me like a pop-up book version of itself, in all its beauty and pomposity. To describe why this city mattered to my brother feels a little like betrayal. We so often love most the parts of people which they work hard to conceal. All I will tell you is that John had been doubted as a child, and when he began his PhD there at the age of twenty-four, there was a neat little *fuck you* in it to anyone who might have been surprised. He also loved learning, the quiet of libraries. When he became ill, he continued his treatment in Oxford, despite moving in with my parents in London. It was a way to keep purchase on his life there, and the possibility of return, a future in which he was well.

I walked down the road, past the halls of residence where he used to live and where we had had his wake: boxed wine and the thought all night that it should be a wedding; the crowd was so young. I missed the Thames and felt confused to be out of the dimensions of nature. The buildings seemed overly tall. A sick feeling came again and again, my stomach contracting painfully.

*

And then there were the cemetery gates.

Portals do appear in our lives, passing places from which we may not return unchanged.

I went in. The path was patterned with dropped leaves. The stone was there, of course, exactly as it was meant to be. It bore the inscription we had asked for:

> *John Beecher*
> *Beloved*
> *14.12.86–12.12.12*

I took off my backpack and sat down on the grass before that striking date of death – no date so uniform possible for another hundred years.

I had printed out a poem before leaving London, '*Demain dès l'aube*' by Victor Hugo, which I now took carefully from the folds of my notebook. It is about walking to a grave and begins:

> Tomorrow at dawn, the moment when the land
>   whitens,
> I will set out. You see, I know that you are waiting
>   for me.

I had walked through six dawns on my path here and felt a new kinship with the land and the river. I had seen it all in so many states of light. What a relief it was now to have Hugo's poem to explain myself to John. It is exhausting always having to make our own language for things.

I read it aloud.

Then I spoke a little to him directly: *Hi, John, I have walked all the way here from home.*

But he was not there. My worry that the grave would be faulty somehow or missing entirely had been an absurd wish. Part of me, I realised, had imagined not this stone but John himself meeting me here, with his slightly sardonic smile. I lay down on the ground and wept.

Eventually, a man approached me. The man's name was Gerry, and he was there to see his wife, Beryl.

You love him, he said simply, when I told him about John.

It takes courage to approach a sobbing stranger and I may admire Gerry, whom I never saw again, more than any other person I have met. He sat with me a long time, then I stayed a little longer alone before taking the train back to London. The journey took less than two hours.

What can be done with love? After a person dies, our bodies can spin with the surplus energy of our unused care. Checking on the gravestone was never my true task. The walk was a container for my love for John, a way to convert that love into effort. It physicalised the distance between us, turned it into a line on a map. It turned it into this story.

After my walk, I kept the river close.

On the South Bank with friends, I would imagine reaching into the Thames, tugging the water like a length of cloth and gathering it into my arms. As long as I lived in London, I thought, I'd always be near it, always connected to John.

But one cannot hold onto water. I didn't know it then, but I'd soon leave the city and the river far behind.

Telling

In Texas I slept beneath the mounted head of a stag, its once-strong neck curving above me in the gloom. San Antonio in August: forty degrees Celsius outside. I was twenty-nine years old and staying in the temporarily empty home of a friend – a former professor of John's my family had become close to following his death. Books in my brother's specialist subjects lined her shelves and awakened a discreet ache within me; wherever I went in the world, there he wasn't.

I had arrived heartsore from the English Man, *bored* of love's messy conclusions. Or to put it another way, I was disappointed and afraid. I was there to work on my novel, having always found it easier to write away from home and all its inevitable little tasks. The apartment was enclosed in a complex behind an electric gate. It was starkly different to my shared house in Virginia, where moths spilled into the kitchen whenever I opened the door of the pantry, and I spent hours wiping away their eggs with a bleach-soaked rag.

*

I did get a lot of work done over my weeks there. Also, alone and unseen, I stopped eating.

Upon arrival, I studied the food in my absent host's kitchen: dozens of tiny cans of prune juice and a few ageing items in the fridge, bendy carrots and olives beginning to lose the firmness of their skin. Without a car, it is often phenomenally difficult to buy food in America and, as I began to strategise about taking a cab up into the city's vast net of overpasses to a grocery store, it occurred to me that I might put my separation – from others and from a ready supply of food – to use. It wouldn't be so bad to eat a little less. I began to look into fasting and found reams of legitimising claims: it would make me more energetic, extend my life and clear my very cells of waste. I was embarrassed to admit, even to myself, that I just wanted to lose weight, but here were all these nobler aims.

It was quick: the way rules bred other rules and my lies to myself became stranger.

The plausibly reasonable *No eating after 5 p.m.* narrowed into a window of a few hours in which I was permitted to eat, before that window narrowed again to a single hour. And I soon began to believe with odd conviction that I had been living in a kind of stupor, sedated by food, and that eating as little as possible was the only way I would access lucid thought.

The joke, of course, is that, when I stopped eating, what I thought about was food. My brain hurried forward towards that hour in which I might eat, what I would allow myself. I became preoccupied with how I would stave off hunger before and afterwards – perhaps carbonated water would help. I tinkered with my rules, debating whether milk in my morning coffee was an infraction. And my mind brimmed with denied pleasures: the soft flesh of fruit around a stone, the savour of buttered bread.

The sky was light pink behind the cacti as I walked the evening streets, my body brittle and resonant from fasting, like an empty glass. I so was ashamed of the thought that I might be lonely.

At night, in that big white bed under the stag, my heart raced as if I were being chased. It took hours to switch off my body and sleep. I'd wake to a headache and the taste of my unbrushed teeth, then the racing would begin again. Fasting was making me anxious; it was undeniable. But, already, I was afraid to stop. Because it was a relief to close off the possibility of food for nearly the entire day. I didn't want to go back out there, into the dangerous space beyond my sanctuary of rules.

In Texas, I did not make a scene one would be horrified to walk in on, there in someone else's bathroom, their perfumes glinting on the sink – though I did spend a lot of time in that room, stepping on and off the scales. I simply remembered a talent for extremity I thought I'd long ago lost. It was a jolting shock, like hearing a voice, hostile and close, in a house where I had believed myself alone.

I am someone who makes sense of life through stories, so it frustrates me that I can't find a beginning for this one. For I have no memory of a time before my body seemed compellingly mutable to me, a thing to be brought to heel.

I do recall standing in a line of little girls in swimming costumes on the edge of a pool and asking each of them how much they weighed, the need to contextualise my own stones and ounces against this information.

I remember how gorgeously adult it felt – aged ten and on a school trip to the Isle of Wight – to tell a friend, *I'm going on a diet*, as we filled glass ornaments with stripes of coloured sand.

I remember the torn photograph of my mum on a beach, from which she had ripped away her own *fat legs*. I remember her comments about herself, which had the tenor of a joke – *Does my bum look big in this?* – albeit one spoken hurriedly before it could be made at her expense; comments that made up part of a tapestry of small insults grown women laid upon their own bodies and each other's, sometimes with naked meanness and sometimes with a confusing sort of camaraderie. I remember going to a party once on the cusp of adolescence where petals of light fluttered over the floor from a disco ball; a woman sprang towards my mum and said, *Nicki, thank God you're here, these young girls are so beautiful, I feel fat and ancient.* I am still angry at this woman for drawing my lovely mother into her kinship of repulsiveness.

I remember unearthing my mum's wedding dress in a cupboard at my grandparents' house at thirteen, trying it on and finding myself unable to do up the zip. It was a brazen challenge to what she'd always told me: my own body was perfect but hers was too big.

I remember two mothers behind the garage in our garden, each with a teaspoon in hand, sharing a tin of condensed milk. Neither was able to keep such a food in their house because of the danger of eating it all. They giggled together, conspirators, performing the fact of their hiding. And I am the girl by the bush of sour-sweet gooseberries, my bare arms ripped by the thorns, learning that food is both a joy and a sin.

And I remember getting older and realising my appearance would matter a great deal to my ambition to be an actor, though, maddeningly, no adult would say it out loud, except the woman at a drama-school audition who told me and the other young hopefuls in that mirrored room, *I have looked at your bodies and I know who I like.*

I have never known how to tell it.

At some point in my teens, I began to diet with punishing zeal, subsisting for a while on soup powder stirred into boiling water or grapefruits and hard-boiled eggs. Sometimes, I'd meticulously count calories until I reached a meagre cap, losing enough weight in a week or two to garner praise from those who noticed. Never enough to provoke concern.

My starvations would eventually induce a kind of bodily panic and I'd begin to eat.

I'd start at the back of the pantry, opening a little bag of peanuts, releasing their oily scent, and counting out ten, and then another ten, and then eating a fistful. The salt I licked from my fingers, the special sting of it in my hangnails, opened a chasm within me and I'd move on to sugary dried fruits, clawing through the muesli for raisins and feeling them plump up within me when they hit the juices of my guts, swelling my hollow stomach. Then I'd pour cereal into a bowl and have it with milk, then drink a bowl of milk, then tear strips of bread from a loaf, dragging them through butter, not bothering with a knife. Knife into the peanut butter, my tongue on the blade. Rice cakes and cottage cheese, those pale dieter's rations, but then – *fuck it* – leftover pasta or cold curry and the glorious depth and colour of real food. A sliced tomato, the slime of the seed part gulped fast into my throat like a still-wriggling fish. All the attempted final bites which only made me hungrier, wet sweetness of fruit, salt crunch of crackers, juice and carrots and olives, the acidity of chocolate, eroding the golden block of palm sugar with a fork. I don't remember the exact circumstances of the first time, only the way panic became a kind of enraged revelry, which gave way to a drugged calm and pacified, methodical chewing, then a terrible engorged pain, not just in my stomach, but all over, as if my very fingertips and neck were also stuffed, then the rise again of panic and the thought that – just this once – it might be best to vomit. It was hard and then surprisingly easy to do.

And to do again the next time.

I never met the diagnostic criteria for bulimia: a certain frequency of bingeing and purging sustained over a certain period. When I came across these numbers at eighteen, they seemed to decree that what I had been doing, though not normal, wasn't truly a problem. Compared to the girls I found online trading tips on which foods expanded in the stomach and which might easily be brought back up, I assessed my own *issue with food* as relatively mild.

And my body barely changed in response to it – just a little sallowness, a slight puffiness to my face, the occasional burst blood vessel staining one of my eyes. Bulimia leaves a trail of tiny marks, which might just be nothing at all.

So, how thin did you get? I was once asked.

Sitting in the passenger's seat in the car park of a Chinese restaurant, I'd tried – mouth clumsy with embarrassment – to explain the bulimic patch of my past to the man beside me.

My answer – *not very* – made the whole story sound like a lie.

But it is a special madness to eat and eat and then vomit, one I have never fully outrun.

Recently, I found myself out of toothpaste and brushed my teeth with baking soda. It lightly burnt my gums, made my teeth feel porcelain-clean and brought back the caustic memory of swallowing it by the spoonful to make myself throw up.

It is like being possessed, when alien thoughts thicken in the mind, and one is forced to contradict one's values, to become an animal, first alert with hunger, then crouched like a cat, whole body up on the kitchen counter, puking into the sink. But possession, while frightening, can be a relief. Restrictive eating fills a day with freighted decisions. Carrying contradiction around fills the mind with chatter, an inner argument to police. It is calming to be out of control.

Bulimia was a room where I could rest.

These periods of possession, when I was hurled into the loop of restriction and release, were always part of a larger loop, which included long stretches where it all mattered far less, and I basically felt sane: a gift that makes this story hard to tell. Instead of mounting, the narrative tension repeatedly falls slack.

At eighteen I failed to get into drama school and spent a season opening rejection letters and crying on the stairs.

Then I moved abroad to work as an au pair, where I had my own flat in a near-derelict building, four floors above my employer's cake shop. The uninhabited rooms around me were stuffed with broken chairs. There was a bathroom sink in the kitchen. The toilet was out in the hall, as was the unlockable shower, which made me feel vulnerable; anyone who entered the building could come up, open the door and find me naked. My cupboards held traces of the last au pair, an American girl who seemed to subsist on pulverised things – Nesquik and a white powder that mixed into a disgusting substance called ranch dressing. I had brought a book with me on cognitive behavioural therapy for bulimia. I can't remember where I got it, only that I read it repeatedly like a catechism and stashed it as secretively as a porn mag.

Living alone frightened me.

'It was a thing that got away from me – a party I threw in a parentless house,' poet Aimee Seu writes of bulimia. I had long dreaded someone coming home to catch me in the heat of a binge, but here nobody would. And I wondered if, in fact, discovery had been what I'd hoped for all along.

There I am, then, in the yellow light of that little flat, eating powdered chocolate milk by the spoonful, dry against my tongue at two in the morning, my back against the fridge, the spell of insatiability over me, when I know this will be the last time.

Quiet dropped around me and I found myself standing on a boundary. The only choices were to give myself over to it completely or give it up. I was nineteen then: the last time I slid the wrong end of a toothbrush into the soft cavern of my throat. Five years after the first time, my pharyngeal wall was well practised, ready to spasm and erase the act of eating.

Bulimia is extremity and violence: the stuff of narrative climax. It is easy to mistake it for the peak of the story and to mistake its cessation for an ending.

What can be said, then, of the ten years that followed?

There were many renunciations. I'd invent intolerances or give things up for Lent, despite having never been religious; I'd cut out sugar, or wheat, or dairy, or all of the above, or breakfast or snacks. I revelled in the plotting this all took, sliding through the ticket barriers in London, smug with denial and intricately planning the dessert of apple slices with a sprinkle of cinnamon I'd gift myself when I got home. Once, I decided to only eat raw foods, and found myself doubled over on a train, my poor stomach twisting with the effort of digesting a feast of uncooked cabbage.

I always told myself that I was not dieting, even when I used an app to fastidiously log everything I ate, my target intake more befitting of a toddler than an adult. Its logo was a silhouette of a person leaping through the air, presumably with the sheer exhilaration of calorific control. If I climbed into bed with hunger nibbling at my empty stomach I'd run my hands lovingly over that stretch of skin, feeling victorious. I'd take hold of my hipbones, as if to anchor myself there. As if my most essential self were my skeleton, not my mind.

For that whole decade I was almost convinced I didn't care about thinness, that I was interested in health and coming into a more monk-like relationship with habit; that all this had something to do with being an artist. And yet, if I caught my reflection in a shop window and saw myself smaller than before, as I once did when hurrying through Croydon in a striped blue dress, I'd have the thrilling sense that I was drawing closer somehow to my real life.

Then I'd put the weight back on.

Weight came and went like weather and so did my interest in it, but what never left was the quiet hum of fear.

Fear of grapes; their musky sweetness was irresistible, and I could only eat them by the bunch until I was swollen and sore – better to never have them at home. Fear of peanut butter. Fear of bread. A subtle dread when confronted by a table of food laid out at a party. And a great fear of cereal, which made me prickle with anger I was too embarrassed to explain when those I lived with brought it into the house.

Eternally embarrassed by my appetite, I stood by the fridge taking mouse portion after mouse portion of food, cutting cold pizza into ribbons with scissors, looking over my shoulder in case anyone entered and witnessed my hunger.

*

Sometimes hunger still took me. It felt awful to polish off a whole container of yoghurt, but it was also soothing, travelling beyond satiety with each cold, white spoonful to that stiller place, the quiet, deep privacy of shame.

It doesn't add up to a story, this interlude between nineteen and twenty-nine, a thing worth wrenching from the body through the throat. It is just a catalogue of wasted thought.

I left Texas diminished.

The pantry moths were still there back in Virginia, the little ghostly fibres of their eggs irremovable from all my food. Friends complimented my weight loss. But my rules couldn't survive re-entry into my usual existence, and my body soon returned to the way it had always wanted to be.

It's not much of a story, I know.

Except those sweltering weeks were a hinge in my life, and afterwards I knew that I was done with dieting forever. I had at last walked enough of that territory to never need to return.

Because it taught me that all my little renunciations had been lies. Some part of me would always want this monster hunger, the kind that undoes the mind, a body enraged – incandescent, a tinnitus high note dimmed only by the white noise of a binge.

Because this time around I was twenty-nine and not nineteen. I was less interested in the fruits of discomfort.

I was not nineteen. And adulthood is a long forever in a parentless house, with no one but myself to stop me.

Because by now, I had seen both a grandmother and a brother grow thinner and thinner until they died. She on her green chair with her legs tucked up, Grandad bearing a potato towards her and saying, *I have to shame her into eating.* John, all bone at the end, elbows sharp and tumour visible through his skin.

And because I too, one day, would be dead.

At the wake for a family friend, a video clip was shown of her frowning at a photo of herself and saying, *I'm fatter there than I am now.* And I wanted to stride back into that past and tell her, *No one has spent this day discussing the time, in your whole beautiful life for which we loved you, when you weighed the least.*

Because it all makes me twitch with *boredom.* Or to put it another way, it fills me with rage.

It was a productive shock, my return to extremity. Texas. Because when that voice, which had been whispering into my ear from before my memory began, grew so loud once again it was unignorable, I could at last turn and tell it to *get out of my house.*

Years ago, a friend knocked on my door in South London. Bulimia had corroded her teeth into fierce little mountains, and as long as I had known her, she had covered her mouth to laugh. Eventually, after years of secret effort, the learning of a whole new way to live, she had contracted a dentist to install veneers at great expense, each individual tooth screwed into place over the old – an extreme measure perhaps for an ordinary, unnoticeable mouth. But I knew about her quietly epic journey towards those teeth, and we both shed a few tears that day in my hallway. *Your beautiful, beautiful teeth*, I said, and we laughed at ourselves for crying.

I have never known how to tell it. But it has done so much for me, being told.

Later, in Virginia, I lived for a while with another recovering bulimic, the poet who wrote of the party in the parentless house. We hardly spoke of it. But there was absolution in knowing that she and I had once done the same strange things in secret.

It is dull and private, the unlearning of fear, hard to dramatise.

You sit in the therapist's office, unspool it.

You tell a partner, properly, for the first time.

When diets take over the conversation with friends, you put in your headphones and feign the urge to get up and sweep the floor.

You find yourself admiring the soft animal of a friend's stomach when her shirt lifts as she reaches to a high shelf for a glass. You wonder how anyone could fault such an innocent thing. And afterwards you carry that stomach, with its three folds, in your mind. A talisman.

You watch the old women in the changing rooms, pool water in their white hair, climbing on and off the scales, and you renew your vow not to let this thing go vining its way along the entire length of your life.

You do the only thing you can with a story of unruly shape, a story without a beginning. You decide and keep deciding. This is how it ends.

Smashed

I first got drunk at thirteen in the upstairs room of a cheap Italian restaurant, sip by sip on other people's wine. I grinned and giggled as the floor lurched, telling my companions, *It's like being on a boat.*

I first got paralytic at thirteen, a few months on. Remembering the pleasant, silly sensation I'd experienced, I went to a party and drank a pint of gin. I soon found myself lying on my back outside, the patio slabs cold beneath my sweating body, urine seeping through my fuchsia combat trousers, slipping in and out of consciousness as the sky span. I was vaguely aware of the kids around me debating whether or not to call an ambulance.

The next day as I walked home, nauseated by my friend's guiding touch, pausing often to retch onto the pavement, I felt grateful that they hadn't called for help, because I wanted to keep what had happened from my parents. They found out anyway, but they didn't tell me off or ask me anything about it. I only remember standing in their bedroom with its huge mirror on the wall, tacks hammered into its frame to hold my mum's necklaces of coloured glass, my dad lifting his eyes to me from the bed to say, disappointed and irritated, *You're too young to be doing this.*

If he had asked me what had happened, I would have been too proud to admit my ignorance. There had been a cluster of bottles at the party and a sheath of plastic cups. I had simply picked a bottle and picked a cup. I had not thought about how different alcohols are drunk in different measures and had not noticed until later that the cups held pints. The worst thing about being a child and then a teenager is the sense that you should know everything already, should never ask, *How am I supposed to do this?* It hardens us, this pretence at wisdom, propelling us towards horrible experiences so that we might reach the knowledge on the other side of them.

Unremarkable: my little body, alcohol rising in my blood. Drinking like this was a fact of the culture, part of passing from childhood to adolescence. And, once I had learnt how to fall only a little way over the edge of it, what freedom it offered.

By fourteen, I understood spirits. I drank vodka, never gin. A friend and I would slip into a secret space behind the apse of a church at the end of my road. She'd withdraw a bottle from her rucksack and the spirit would travel down our throats, sharp and straight as a sword swallower's blades. We'd savour the burn of it, of being there alone together, doing unseen what was not allowed. Then we'd run, feral and clumsy, down one steep hill and up another to meet the rest of our crowd, the running magically easy, our lungs so much stronger than when we were sober. We would stand around the swings where we had flown as children, sailing out beyond our bodies for one suspended moment before we fell back into our bones. We drank to exit childhood and to hold onto it, to slip out of our terrible self-consciousness and play a little longer in the park. Night over us, we stumbled through that other gateway into adulthood, the one marked, *Sex*.

There were drunk kisses. The bravery to lean towards another person, to try for contact. The blot of shame when it wasn't reciprocated blurred away by the next morning's headache. There was drunk touch and drunk sex – was there any other type of sex to be had? At fifteen my body made a bolt for womanhood. Suddenly, grown men looked at me differently and I was the one sent into the off-licence; drink and sex fed from one another's hands. But subtler knots formed in me too, between freedom and danger, joy only to be granted with a loss of control, all the lovely, awful things that happened in the dark.

There I am with my friends at the drained reservoir on the edge of town. Night has come and licked our shadows from the grass and spirits have stripped and lit up our insides. We're on a makeshift beach surrounded by woods. Through our talk and singing we begin to hear a sound in the dark. We shush each other to listen. It is the steady beat of a drum. Our confusion becomes fear as the beat grows louder and louder, closer and closer, until we scream and scatter between the trees. And then there is young men's laughter and the horror movie ends. Slipping out from our hiding places, we find the boys from the year above, all beauty and menace. And what pleasure there was in being chosen to be menaced, the warm moment after the chill of fear.

I hoped to be chosen. And to escape the exposure of making choices. Drink created a second self to blame if you did something embarrassing or prohibited, and in this way you never had to account for your desire. This did not mean you wouldn't be held accountable by others; there was much ritual shaming, reserved exclusively, of course, for girls. But you could, and we did, say *but I was drunk*.

There I am on holiday at fifteen, waking naked in a tent with a man in his twenties, the line of a sleeping-bag zip pressed into my skin, and only vague, swirling images of the night before: sitting around a fire, the young man I liked more than the one I woke up with pressing his lips to a gas canister and releasing propane into his mouth.

There I am inside the metal train in the children's playground, drink erasing the world beyond us so this small, cold space feels private, a body on top of mine and me still new to this, bunching my top in my hands against the pain.

There I am, the lovely dark nipple of another girl in my mouth, in love but never naming it, falling asleep with our legs interlocked.

When the get-out clause *but I was drunk* finally failed, and I was driven out of school as a dyke and a slut, I still whispered it to myself, clenching its small protection inside my own fist.

When I moved to London at sixteen, the friends I found there never stood in a circle passing the vodka. We sometimes shared cheap pink wine in each other's back gardens and sometimes went to bars, but it was not the urgent, obliterative sort of drinking I had gone along with before. What a relief. And yet our sexuality still shone brightest when we ordered Smirnoff Ices in tawdry nightclubs, pulling the disguise of confidence over our faces, hoping not to be ID'd. I look back and cringe and love us for all those nights spent at Soho gay bars, grinding on each other, our sexuality enacted with awkward exuberance to the sound of Britney Spears.

And then I was an adult, being photographed by my dad on my eighteenth birthday buying my first legal pint. Around this time, I broke up with my first boyfriend and he drank an entire bottle of Cointreau, then stained my parents' sofa with saccharine orange vomit. *What an idiot*, I thought. But I understood the romance in the impulse, the desire to make things loose and grand and cinematic rather than just sad.

It was clear to me that I wasn't *a drinker*. My life wasn't bound to the rhythm of big nights and rough mornings. Two beers were often enough to send me to sleep. But I did meet a drinker and fall in love with him. Our first date was in a wood-panelled pub, the chatter rising around us so we had to lean in closer to hear each other's voices. I remember seeing my face in the scratched mirror in the toilets, that moment of confirmation – *Girl, you are drunk* – before I went downstairs. We ducked out together for cigarettes, then kissed for the first time on the pavement. He bought beers at Waterloo Station afterwards and said, *Carling, darling?* as he pulled me a can from the six-pack. I was nineteen. I stayed with him for seven years.

Throughout our relationship, *Carling Darling* would disappear. Once we lived together, he would occasionally leave our flat on a Friday and not return until late on Sunday night, blank and twitchy from beer and lack of sleep, smelling vinegary with booze and stale sweat, his phone long dead. Eventually I put my number on a scrap of paper in his wallet, with the instruction written beneath it in my clearest hand, *Please don't forget I exist.* All our holidays would be marked by his absences. He'd stay out, *just for one more*, and I would lie awake as the hours unfurled in a hostel in some warmer part of the world, watching lizards on the ceiling and thinking, *I hope he is alive.* He always rolled in eventually, full of dull tales. Compared to him, I barely drank at all.

I didn't have it: the switch labelled *More*, which would flick within him after a drink or two.

And yet, at twenty-six, when I walked into a party and saw someone else, it was intoxication, the pink glow of it, the feeling of slipping from my usual skin, that allowed me to kiss that stranger, a dark-haired man from Streatham Common. I became *besotted* with him: a word that once meant drunk and now means blindly adoring. Soon after that night, I left *Carling Darling* and our whole imagined shared future.

Newly single, I entered a second adolescence of sorts at twenty-six, another chance at exploration, want suddenly so awake in me once more.

There I am, the alcohol scent of hairspray in a cloud about my face, perfume on my wrists, my neck, out to meet the man from Streatham Common, of course at a pub.

And there I am, drinking whisky with a different stranger, our hands on the table as if by chance, a crackle of electricity when his knuckles graze the backs of my fingers.

There I am at the Edinburgh Fringe, with a woman I have flirted with all year, bold enough at last to bring her back to my single bed at the end of a raucous night; in the small hours she stumbles, lithe and half naked, through the flat to the surprise of my housemates.

There I am, flying over guy ropes at a different festival, landing hard and pulling a man down with me, him younger, tight blonde curls across his head like a newly shorn lamb, the ground holding us, grass tickling my neck and the backs of my arms as I look past him at the stars.

Drink was a quieter companion now than it had been in my teens. Because I never ended the night vomiting over the side of a bridge, because I still couldn't keep pace drink for drink with so many of my friends and often found myself searching the cupboards at parties for the things to make a cup of tea with, it never occurred to me that it was always there. But it was. And it was part of the fun of these encounters, which opened a magic realm for me, a space beyond bereavement.

People talk about drink *taking the edge off,* but I have also found it to sharpen things, making desire a bright-rimmed object one might reach out and grab.

Yet there is sadness in this magic.

Things happened that my sober self would not have wanted to happen. Once with a woman – in the toilets of a theatre, a wine glass smashing into the sink, a mouth on my body I did not ask for – and once with a man. Old enough to know better, I drank some luminous knock-off absinthe and woke with my head and stomach stormy. My body brimmed with the kind of rotting heat that makes compost bins catch fire. Someone was there; I felt a breath on my back, the acid-sweet-stale breath of a person who has been drinking. I turned and saw a man in my bed. A friend who others thought of as handsome, though he had only seemed abstractly so to me. I had a white duvet embroidered with elephants, and there was a small amount of blood on it. And gone, as if removed from my brain in a perfect orb with an ice-cream scoop, was the memory of how we had got there. All day I scrambled for it, the way I had frantically checked every pocket for my phone after I was pickpocketed on the bus, already knowing it was irretrievably lost. I visited my mum that morning and found myself sobbing like a child. Now, closer to thirty than thirteen, I could admit my ignorance; I had drunk more than my body could understand and a lonely thing had taken place.

But this is the cliché of mixing sex and alcohol: girl gets too drunk; regrets. The loneliest moments, I think, are the ones that, in a 3 a.m. sort of way, seem to be something like love. The New Year's Eve when that man from Streatham with whom I had become so besotted arrived on my doorstep, his mouth at last full of *I love you*. I had ached to hear it, and this would be the only time he ever said it in this way, the words emerging, unequivocal and unbidden, not a response to me, not a *Well, I love you too but* . . . He said it again and again. But in the morning he was in pain, hurt by the light that came in through my window, too nauseated to be touched. And he couldn't remember a word he'd spoken.

It is not that situations augmented with alcohol aren't real, it is that they come with get-out clauses: *I don't recall, I didn't mean it.* The old excuses of the second self.

A few years ago, two friends each told me, separately and many times, that they really should not have sex with one another despite a mutual attraction. One was in a relationship. The other knew it would hurt more than it was worth. At a party, as we danced around the ankle-breaker of a broken vent in the living-room floor, I watched them pour drink after drink, until what they wanted was inevitable. For a while I attempted to honour their earlier pleas of *just don't let me* by distracting them. At one inventive moment, I suggested we all pretend to be weasels. But I knew all was lost when she turned to him, her dark pupils enlarged, poured another and asked, *Do you believe in God?* I went to bed. They knew that their drunk selves could do what their sober selves could not, and they were determined to conjure them, shot by shot.

At twenty-nine, I had a *new* new boyfriend, the English Man I had met in my first weeks in the US. He was kind and strangely formal and neat, like a Brit conjured by American imagination. I confided in my friend Katie that, terribly, I kind of preferred him when he was drunk. He seemed to animate then, burning bright and available, undoing his collar and becoming sillier, less sad. One night we returned to my apartment from a party dressed as pirates. We put on doo-wop songs and yelled all the *I love you*s into each other's faces while dancing around my shabby furniture. I mistook it for something really being said.

But he didn't love me. He loved 3 a.m., breaking out of his usual stiffness and buttoned-up shirts. He loved waking the neighbours. When I realised this, my heart broke, *again*. Oh well, I thought, if I would insist on flinging it around.

It is such an embarrassment, longing. I see it all clearly now. In my teens, as I yanked myself gracelessly out of childhood, alcohol freed and masked my desire. I could pretend that sex just happened to me; it was not a product of my own curiosity, my want. In my twenties it offered me flashes of intimacy, which felt like strange, blurry accidents: shadow tenderness, which vanished when the light changed. The need to disguise my desire for sex had transformed into a need to disguise my desire for love.

So many of my shocks, my little epiphanies, are mundane like this: *Ah, yes, I see now that in this small way I have failed to be brave.*

I never exactly decided to stop meeting lovers at parties or bars, possibility glinting along the edge of the phrase, *Do you want another drink?* I just stopped going out. When the English Man and I broke up, I found myself disinterested in the pain. *Yes, yes,* I thought as I stomped through the following days, impatient for time to get to work in me. I made a list called *Things That Help* (sunlight, human contact, reading, sleep), and treated it like a prescription. A short time later I could joke with him, *You broke my heart, but I knew how to fix it.* It was true. Also true: a small but keen-eyed creature within me, my instinct towards partnership, had retreated or perhaps died. I was tired. Men had disappointed me and with women I had disappointed myself, never been sure-footed enough.

At home in London that summer, I snapped at my mother in the park when she said, *You just know when you meet the one.* Everyone who said that, I told her, had met their spouse by twenty-five. That year, I had won a lump of money for a short story I'd written, and I now spent long hours with my laptop open at night trying to work out whether it would be enough to freeze my eggs, what that would entail and how much it would hurt.

I returned to America and stayed a while in a friend's apartment taking care of their dog, a sweet mongrel rescue who could not unlearn hunger and would tear the place apart, ripping open packets of dry spaghetti if left alone for long. When I took her out, strangers complemented her beauty. I felt compelled to tell them she wasn't mine.

Six months before I had met a man at a Chanukah party – a cold night in a crowded room, candles doubling in the rain-spattered windows. I told him I liked his woolly jumper; he thanked me and said it was from Iceland. I must have learnt his name, though I forgot it, and him, until we met again. It was – and is – Luke. By chance, I discovered that he lived close to the dog's owners, making us temporary neighbours. Somehow, we decided that he should come along on my next dog walk.

It did not feel momentous to come out of the apartment on that first afternoon and see him waiting a little way down the street for us in a dip between hills. The dog strained on her leash and down we went to meet him. As we walked, we passed a burnt house, tall and torn open, its blackened insides essentialised by fire, the image slightly unreal, like a woodcut in a picture book. We looped streets and weedy alleyways, gardens of late irises and roses, until the dog abruptly threw herself down in some grass, panting, refusing to move. And now the

heavy symbol, which really was there: someone had painted a huge white love heart on the grass. Luke and I sat
above it, talking with a rare kind of ease, which I should
have taken notice of. Still, the words from that afternoon
in my notebook: *It is interesting to make a completely
platonic friend.* We kept taking walks, just the two of us,
after the dog's owners returned. And without considering
what it meant, I began to feel like I wanted to see him
every day.

The verbs of falling in love speak of a tricking sort of
magic. We are beguiled or charmed or *besotted*. I did
not recognise this unfamiliar thing, this drawing closer
unaided, no change in state but each other, the instinct
to reach for his hand. That summer I moved with Katie
and two other friends to a magnificent, dilapidated house
with a pillared front porch and squirrels living in the
walls. Its entrance was tangled with vines. Katie found
me singing and joyfully leaping about in our living room
one afternoon as I waited for Luke to arrive to take me
swimming in a pool in the woods. *Anna, if this isn't a date,*
she asked, *why are you so excited?*

I have kissed many people. As a teenager, I kept their
names on a list, shaping the letters carefully in smooth
gel pen. As an adult, I held my kisses as memories in my
muscles and nerves, a collage of faces. In my long eras of
monogamy, I missed first kisses, the lambent moments
when flirtation crystalised into something undeniable.

I first kissed Luke at dusk by a stream after we swam in the woods. Dragonflies shadowed over the water. Because we were sober, we did not crash together. He asked, softly, *Do you mind if I touch you?* How rarely anyone has asked. He stroked my arms and my back. My excitement did not feel laced with confusion or threat. I had always thought of flirting as the casting of a spell, a sequence of gestures, phrases and tricks, to make one's dull self momentarily gorgeous. By this definition we had not been flirting. And yet, something between us had become undeniable. We moved through the gateway of our first kiss, slightly awkwardly, at least one of us with bad breath.

Later, I racked my mind for another sober first kiss and could think only of my first ever kiss, aged twelve, which took place, as the rhyme goes, *sitting in a tree* with a tall blond boy, our legs dangling over the branch and the whiff of chlorine still on us from the swimming pool. Between this kiss and my first kiss with Luke lies the length of an entire childhood, eighteen years.

I did not know that I was falling in love with Luke until it had already, irrevocably happened, altering forever the course of my life. After that kiss, we could not easily turn back. Whatever came next, the moment could not be cleared away – *I don't remember, I didn't mean it* – like bottles at the end of a night.

There can be beauty in intoxication, in slipping out of the daily self beneath a wide, dark sky, revelling, human and ancient, staggering a little against the spin of the Earth. But beautiful, too, is reality. Walking through the woods with senses sharp. Coming to the place where the stream pools and choosing that wild water. Letting its cold blaze through us. How the skin sings afterwards, utterly awake.

Part 2

Holler

Holler

(noun) *A small, sheltered valley between mountains* (dialect; Southern US, Appalachia; variant of *Hollow*)

Apocalypse

In the frigid January of 2018, I had planned to meet my mum and brother Max in New York, when a weather phenomenon I had never heard of hit the city. The phrase *bomb cyclone* sounded like American hyperbole, until my flight from Virginia was cancelled and then so was the train, and I found myself on a freezing Greyhound bus inching haltingly through the dark. The governor of Virginia had declared the weather a state of emergency and in New York it was worse, the wind racing down the long, straight streets at thirty miles an hour. Piles of snow bordered the roads, mountainous and glinting, some of them splashed with colour by illuminated signs. My phone was a glowing rectangle in the dim bus as I tracked by turn my own location and then my Mum and Max's flight from London, which was late but airborne.

It had been six months since I'd moved to the US, my longest ever separation from my family. We should have abandoned our plan to meet in light of the forecast but could not; we were so determined to defy the distance between us, to make *See you in New York* an ordinary thing, like the *See you at Sheffield Bus Station* of our past.

91

I kept playing Paul Simon's 'Mother and Child Reunion' through my headphones that night, the title phrase dancing through me down the dark highways as I drew closer to my mum. I wanted to send her the song but doubted her ability to work Spotify on her phone. Besides, I knew that the lyrics, which made me so happy, would only make her sad.

In New Jersey, I dashed out and swapped my bus for a train. Somehow snow was falling on the inside, gathering on the floor in the articulated chambers between carriages. I refreshed the page on my phone and discovered that their flight had landed but five hundred miles away from New York in North Carolina. After much calling, my mum was remarkably cheerful when I finally got through to her. *A lovely woman has cracked open her duty free!* she yelled into the phone.

I had come through New York when I'd arrived in America the previous summer, my shoulders high from carrying my cases, and had visited once before that. Tonight, as the weather infiltrated the train, making it feel dogged and undefended, the thousands of lights that formed the shining face of the city were both muted and made more brilliant by the snow. My body braced as I stepped off the train into Penn Station – a reflexive guard against the cold. All I had felt upon my other arrivals here intensified. My sense of my own smallness, and of New York as not a centre but an edge, an unlikely fortification against the wildness of the Hudson. My ambivalent love of cities seemed concentrated in this one: their harsh, exciting promise of anonymity, their polluted, belching, destructive, ambitious humanity a thing to despair at – though I never truly could, the squash of assembled lives making me tender and, despite everything, hopeful.

I left the station in search of the hotel where we'd all share a room, our budget being more in line with Sheffield Bus Station than New York. The snow fell thickly in diagonal drifts, already covering earlier attempts to clear the road, its asphalt bone far below the surface, snow compacted over it as if by a tank. I was in Manhattan, but the city was almost deserted, with just me and two strangers making our careful way, not a vehicle in sight. It was a vision of crisis, but right then it was wonderful, like all this crazy beauty was a secret just a few of us were in on.

My mum and Max arrived the next day on a rescheduled flight, and we began our obdurate attempt at tourism. It was minus sixteen degrees Celsius in the streets. I wore two coats and tucked a hot-water bottle into the waistband of my trousers, pinking the skin of my stomach. The water had frozen midstream in the fountains as if bewitched, and in Central Park footsteps crisscrossed the lakes. I photographed Max, a delicate silver frost of eye make-up below their winter hat, eating a pretzel from a street vendor, both of us with shaking hands. Outside the New York Public Library, an ice skater span; dressed in black, they made an elegant column against all the white.

*

Though she was determinedly cheerful on that trip, my mother's thoughts circled endlessly back to death. On the A Train and in the Rockefeller Center, where we only visited the lobby because it was too expensive to go up for the view, and in a gold-hued cocktail bar in Grand Central Station and in the National Museum of the American Indian, and in the Slipper Room, where our performance-artist friend Julie lay back in the splits and made peanut butter sandwiches on her crotch, and before the cabinet containing the original Winnie-the-Pooh animals, dishevelled by love, in the New York Public Library, she spoke of what had happened to John, in lines which were always the same. And I replied as I had been doing for years.

I still feel guilty that I didn't believe it, she would say. I'd sometimes reply, *You were trying to be strong for him,* though more and more often I just said, *I know.* Of her own recent cancer, she would only say, *I still feel guilty that I got better when he didn't.* We sailed slowly near the Statue of Liberty in a bitter wind. *I feel so bad for you two,* she said. Max and I met eyes as I said, *I know,* and we shared the thought, *but we're on the fucking Staten Island Ferry.*

One of her legs had swollen since her flight, a side effect of the removal of lymph nodes, but she feigned a lack of concern, sweeping her hand through the air above her head with *pshhh* uttered on the outbreath – a gesture I knew well. At night she would wake in the hotel bed we were sharing, gasping for air, then whisper so swiftly that it was almost the same moment, *I'm all right.*

I wanted to cry out, *Mummy*, but I have always called her by her real name.

Demeter's grief for her daughter Persephone reordered life on Earth, the leaves torn down from the branches, snow falling upon a world that had never seen it. But if it happened the other way around, the mother grabbed by Hades in a cornfield and whisked to the underworld, it would not matter that no one knew how to survive winter, how to preserve heat or fruits and vegetables in jars, because Persephone would not have been permitted to react like that. A whole new season cannot be wrought by a child's yearning to keep a parent in the world.

I thought of the ancient myth in those days of extravagant winter in New York, the snow pouring into the mouths of subways, orbs of warm light glowing weakly through it atop green lampposts at each entrance. The stillness when it stopped. I had never known how ill my mother was, only that three years after John died, cancer grew in her too, in the place, in fact, where he had grown, side by side with Max, and where I had grown also. Its presence was revealed by small dots of blood in her underwear, a sprinkle of red seeds through the white. I had only known the sweep of her hand through the air above her head, *pshhh*, no need for concern.

An image held in amber: my mum in her old house in Sheffield with a glowing pendant amid the moles and sunspots on her chest. She bends low and her red-and-white skirt spreads on the floor. She reaches into the filing cabinet where, in a questionable attempt at organisation, she is storing her utensils, and retrieves a spoon from the drawer marked *S*. How light this person seems, her body and family intact. When I lived briefly in Austria at eighteen, she came to visit, sweating her way through the airport with the extra tops and leggings she'd bought for me layered beneath her clothes. I cried my eyes out when she left, racked with sobs in a public toilet until a kind woman pressed tissues gently into my hands: a moment almost delicious in recollection because my young self had no clue of the things yet to happen. How I'd one day sob again in public but because my brother was dying, and a stranger would appear once more to touch me lightly and say, *It will be all right.* What a kindness, though they were wrong.

In a French café, which was open despite the killing cold outside, my mum giggled with Max and me about the statuesque attractiveness of all the waiters. I knew a kind of end-of-the-world had happened to her. She had lost none of her determination to reach me wherever I was upon the planet, to feed me and wrap me into an extra coat, but her repetitions of grief and guilt thickened the air between us. Trudging through the snow together, the burn of cold wind across our faces and the surfaces of our eyeballs, I thought, *Ask me more about my life.* During that trip, a petulant sense gathered within me that it would cost me something irretrievable to just listen and be kind.

I may have been right, but I regret terribly the words, *You're more interested in your dead child than in me*, uttered in a restaurant where, exhausted from the cold, the three of us shared a disappointing plate of cheese.

Two years later, she came to New York again. It was the cusp of spring. I took the train from Virginia and waited on a corner to receive her from the airport, my attention sharpening with canine eagerness at every cab that went past. Until I moved very far from home, I did not know about the way the physical presence of those we love can feel at once affirming and surreal. When she finally stepped out of a yellow cab, four feet ten in the enormous street, the whole busy world lurched around her before righting itself, settling in a position minutely more correct.

I was six months married. Two summers before I had sat on a concrete wheel stop in a shadeless parking lot and uttered the light cliché into the phone, *I've met someone.* There must have been enough hope in my voice to frighten her, because in one breath she said, *Oh-God-is-he-American-you're-going-to-stay-there-forever-I'm-joking-I'm-joking.* I likely said, *We'll see.* But he was and I had since begun living in this country in a way that I thought of as *forever for now.* I had dug holes in the ground around the house in Virginia I shared with Luke, my new husband, and dropped bulbs into them, pale, fleshy tulips and daffodils like little paper fists. The tips had come up curved and neat as filed green nails and now they waited in bud for me to come home to.

It was March of 2020. At the Museum of Modern Art, we lingered before an image of a veiled woman on green-slippered tiptoes pulling along a unicorn, the crowd ebbing and swelling around us. In a theatre, our voices joined the collective murmur, which hushed as the lights dimmed. A woman in a bar offered us her half-finished bottle of wine, and it tasted crisp and expensive. In a dark Georgian restaurant the tables were crammed so close that we sat inches from the couple beside us, seemingly a professor and his gorgeous student, who frequently leant over their dinners to kiss. There was a birthday party just beyond them, loud with laughter, candlelight moving across the gathered faces. These moments come back to me with the same fast-burning brilliance as the strips of magnesium my brothers once liberated from a classroom, which flared with a white intensity that felt like magic.

This was the week in which the Covid-19 pandemic went from being a curiosity to a crisis. As the days passed, the museums shut and then the theatres, spaces we had just occupied closing over behind us. CNN looped increasing panic into our hotel room. We avoided handrails and pushed lift buttons with sleeves over our fingers. We wondered if we should be wearing masks and where one would even get such a thing. And we laughed and rolled our eyes, because we didn't know how else to react, unpractised as we were at anything like this. Holing up in our hotel room struck us as melodramatic, an overblown surrender to misery. It seemed increasingly wrong to be there, tourists in a city shutting down. But we also felt lucky. Soon we'd be an ocean apart. Who knew when we'd next be able to sit together, our hands travelling easily across the table to try food from one another's plates?

By our final night in New York many establishments had closed, leaving the few restaurants and bars that were still open to punctuate the streets, bright and clamorous between their silent neighbours. As we looked for somewhere to eat, I wanted to call out, *We don't live here, we don't have homes to hide in*, to anyone who might judge us. We had not yet learnt to fear Covid enough to spend our last night in Manhattan perched on hotel sheets eating sandwiches for dinner, confined like the grizzly bear in Central Park Zoo, sleeping with her belly to the sky, too big for her tight quarters. And so, for one more day, we chose to not quite believe it and got drunk together in a flea-bitten bar in Chelsea.

In its dingy backroom, I was more worried about bedbugs than the respiratory droplets of strangers, hovering on the corner of a wooden bench instead of sitting in an armchair, placing my bag on the table carefully, not allowing it to touch anything soft. I listened as my mum began to talk about John.

This is how grief progresses. The dead are no less present, but we learn to share them more carefully. We had waited until the last moment to do this, keeping him at bay all week, though I knew we had both thought of him privately often. And she said what she always says: *I still feel guilty that I didn't believe it, I still feel guilty that I got better when he didn't.* But now, I was thirty-one. My brother had been dead eight years and I had begun to accept my mother's circles of speech.

Once, on a tour of the Vatican, I had watched a line of people in St Peter's Basilica waiting patiently for their turn to kiss or touch the statue of that saint. His stone keys, each fold of his clothing and the ridges and knuckles of his raised hand were rendered in detail, but one of his feet was worn smooth, looking more like a beak or fin, at the bottom of his robes. I was there with a boyfriend who was devoutly anti-religious, and I was embarrassed by my desire to join the queuers. But when he went off to find the loo, I darted to the back of the line, hoping to reach the holy foot before he came back. My palm met the stone, and it was full of gathered warmth. Did it cool overnight, I wondered, then spend the day warming up again with each touch or kiss planted upon it? Repeated touch dulls an object, wearing away its contours, but also imbues it with a kind of charge.

On my mum's side of the family, everyone repeats themselves, their anecdotes as strong and soft as worn-in leather, their hands laid frequently upon certain memories to check they are still there. I find it lightly maddening, but it probably made a storyteller of me. My time as a quiet little witness, up too late at my grandma's table as she told *again* of the ghost of a girl appearing at the end of her bed, was an introduction to the way the atmosphere in a room can alter around a tale, and it was repetition that revealed the crossing-over from conversation into craft. We collude in the re-sharing of stories in this branch of my family, prompting each other with questions. It is like singing a song we all know the words to.

In this bar in this city we were not from, on the cusp of global lockdown, we drank prosecco and I sang along as my mum ushered John up in well-worn words. We laughed once more at his sarcastic claim to have inherited from her *being short, dyslexia and looking like a monkey.* The language was stale but some piece of the pain still fresh as she spoke of thinking in the hospice, *He's looking a bit better.* Moroccan lamps dimmed and scattered the light above our heads and the group beside us grew louder as they drank. That night we had pasta and wine and finished with chocolate cake. We cried a bit. I told her that if I ever seemed a little hard, it was because I had had to be hard. I was twenty-three when John died. I had so much of my life left. I had to steel myself and find something to do with it.

What I did not say was, *I want new songs.* That is what I am doing here in America, wanting and making new songs.

In the hotel that night I lay awake for hours while my insomniac mother slept. There is a notion that when one person sleeps badly, others sleep well; some primal part of us relaxes with someone on guard through the night. I had spent the night in John's hospital room once, days before he died, the tiny lights of the machines piercing the gloom. I felt like his guardian, ready when he woke breathless to pass him an oxygen mask and help him fasten it to his face. Sharing his room was ordinary, like my sleeping on the floor by his bed when visiting his student flat, or the childhood holidays when we'd woken together, hot and cramped in the nest of our family tent. But it felt sickeningly wrong because he was dying and nobody could stop it. In New York my mum snored and I read the news on my phone, worry rising in me about the thought of her journey home, how she would pass through an airport and then sit on a plane, *breathing* all the while. She left at 5 a.m. I turned on CNN and let its doom wash over me as at last I slept.

It was hot on the way to Penn Station, a sudden burst of summer in March that made me stop in the street to peel off my coat and jumper. In the daytime, the city seemed more like itself. There were people everywhere and stores open all along the street, decked beneath bright awnings with fruits and flowers. The sky was hazy; cabs and cars and buses dusted invisible particulate over flower petals and pomegranates and small yellow mangoes. A woman came from behind, striding past me down the street, strong and broad-shouldered, in what looked like the over-washed cotton of hospital clothes. Her hair was wild, and she was raving but deeply focused. *Touch my fucking vagina*, she yelled, *I will kill you*, repeating the phrase with variations, spitting out *touch me* like a dare. The New Yorkers avoided her without visibly stepping out of her way – a coolness I recognised from London. She moved up ahead of me with remarkable speed, so as I walked, I caught the mumbled comments and raised eyebrows of people coming in the opposite direction. In the station I spotted her once more, barrelling around the concourse in loops. *Oh, boy*, said the guy at the bagel shop, smiling wearily, *here she comes again*. Her words were like chunks of hurled masonry – *touch my vagina, I will kill you*. The crowds gave her space, this parody of madness, like a thing spewing sparks, but refused to witness her with more than a glance.

It struck me that I was behaving myself as the pandemic swept towards me, that almost everyone was, keeping our visible reactions small. I was not screaming and yelling. But I was afraid. In a pharmacy, I found the shelf empty of the disinfectant I had hoped to spray around myself on the train. I sighed and bought some gum. How polite fear makes itself when there's nothing to be done.

The train was full. I dowsed my hands and the fold-out table with my last drops of sanitiser and turned my face away from the stranger beside me.

Across the wetlands between New York and New Jersey, light touched the reeds. Egrets alighted and took flight, and other birds I had no names for. *Where am I?* I wondered between stations. The bridges were a Statue of Liberty shade of green. We passed through Philadelphia and Baltimore, places I only knew from cream cheese and television. A tunnel absorbed us in momentary night. There was so much I didn't understand.

*

The first time I took this train it was towards a place I had never seen. The day before it had become a news story, the site of a killing, a brief nexus of right-wing hate. I spent the journey reading tweets about the white-supremacist rally in Charlottesville, looking out of the window *at America*, and drinking coffee from the café car, which had an old-cigarette staleness I had long equated with adventure. When I got off the train, I thought, *I live here*, as I climbed down the steel steps into the sun. I didn't know anyone there and my apartment was not ready (as it still wouldn't be when I moved in, a dot of blood in the freezer and someone else's dark hairs still clinging to the sides of the bath), and so I spent my first night in Charlottesville on a hotel bed watching the fear and outrage on the news. The alarm was all in my brain rather than my body, but when I slipped outside, I jolted horribly at the foreign sight of a possum, its face bright white in the dark of a hedge. The next day, I met a chatty woman in the breakfast room who had flown in from Cleveland because of what had happened, here *to minister and spread love*. At home I'd have thought her a busybody, but foreigners have the luxury of taking people at their word. The woman hugged me, though we'd just met, right there by the waffle iron, with its drips of batter and smell of singed sweetness. I'd stepped right into the America of my imagination: sugar and overfamiliarity. I wondered what the spreading of her love would look like, whether she'd find people who felt that she, in her oversized blue T-shirt printed with the name of her church, was what they needed. But I appreciated her hug, some small piece of mother in it.

What was it like, I wondered, to move so boldly towards other people's pain?

Holler

By our first pandemic summer, we had developed habits. Hand sanitiser no longer reminded me of NHS corridors, of dispensing it, cool and vodka sharp, onto my palms while arranging my face for a death bed. We kept a bottle in the car and globbed it on warm from the Virginia heat. We no longer forgot our masks, and in the supermarket we moved deftly around strangers, avoiding eye contact, as if sharing a glance were sharing air. We had acquired an appetite for brutal, salacious fairy tales and read *The Arabian Nights* aloud in bed. Time had hung slack all spring, our neighbourhood muted yet cacophonous with birds, but by summer it seemed a little tauter. We only occasionally froze in the middle of the living-room carpet, unable to believe it, the day a blank cloth between us.

Luke and I had been married less than a year. Just that September we had stood outside the courthouse, Captain Marshall beaming over us with a star on his jacket and gun on his thigh, vows falling around our shoulders like light. And when the pandemic struck, I was grateful for the way that act had closed the question of where my home was. Marriage quietens the clamour of our possible lives, and this felt more like a gift than a cost in 2020, a smooth pebble of reality when reality seemed so diffuse. I was an alien in this country, awaiting status, but I had chosen Luke and America and its particular chaos.

We broke our isolation once to join a protest. Luke was alert, his hand tightening around mine as we approached downtown Charlottesville. I told him we could go home and make donations, protest without standing in the street, but then there we were – familiarity and shock – close to strangers. George Floyd's face, printed again and again, swayed above us on placards and people chanted the terrible three words he'd uttered as a police officer knelt on his neck. It was sad and beautiful and frightening to be with so many other people, sharing gestures; we followed the crowd, and the concrete was warm when we knelt. And I wondered, as I often do in my adopted country, who among us had a gun.

That June, fireworks went off every night. *It feels threatening*, Luke said, as we lay in bed listening to the explosions, and I thought back to the war I had idly imagined when deciding to live here, a hypothetical nightmare of England sealed away from me. I had never pictured a catastrophe so static, afternoons spent in the basement in a red double sleeping bag, watching the goings-on at a dodgy tiger sanctuary on Netflix. There was no shortage of brutality in the air. In Luke's home state of Michigan, armed protesters had stormed the capitol building, screaming into the faces of the guards, returning weeks later to stand around outside in the drizzle, automatic weapons slung over their plastic ponchos. Elsewhere, Black Lives Matter protesters had been tear-gassed. But the truth was, this all only obliquely touched us. Inside the boundary of our small life, the days were hushed and thin. The summer of 2020 reminded me of later grief, the period after the shock of loss. It is hard to write about because it looks like nothing from the outside, just swiping deodorant onto the armpits and living another day.

A kind of homesickness unfurled the longer we stayed at home. Mine was for England, for the landscape of my own accent, for my parents and brother Max and my ninety-year-old grandfather, who wrote me biro letters on translucent paper and had begun to eat very little, after reading about an experiment with rats who displayed remarkable longevity when underfed. The US border was closed to British nationals. If I left, I might not be re-admitted and all the plants I had seeded in Virginia would spring up with violent speed, then dry to death untended. Both Luke and I were homesick for the old dimensions of life, for touch, small exchanges with strangers, days in which anything might happen.

Eventually we got in our car and went somewhere else. Because driving for seven hours is nothing at all in this country and because travel can be its own type of homegoing, in the same way that passing through a dream can.

It was surreal to leave the meagre territory of our white wood-panelled house and the surrounding streets, to find that so much world was still out there as we made our way across Virginia towards Kentucky, with our tent and stove and plastic box of pans and plates rattling in the back.

Back in 2017, when I still thought myself a visitor to the United States, a friend had invited a group of us to Thanksgiving in her hometown of Jonesboro, Arkansas, which I only knew of, in some compartment of my mind, as the site of a school shooting. We left Charlottesville before dawn and drove until after dark, covering more than eight hundred miles in twelve hours, almost all on a single road. When we at last got out of the car, I felt nausea and the particular exhaustion of having sat still for an entire day, but also a bizarre joy. There I was, a person who had seen death, with so many days at my disposal that I might use a whole one up like this, simply rolling forwards through space. I had an exhilarating sense of *feeling my life*, the long rope of it, which is entirely different from *feeling alive*. I had not met Luke yet and was in fact in love with someone else on that trip to Arkansas, a person who would soon fall from my life completely, as if I had never watched the light touch his sleeping face as we passed the shimmering rim of Nashville. We made wishes that day, holding our breaths over the Frisco Bridge, and I briefly wished to stay with this person, before substituting that for the wish to publish my first novel: a thing I wanted more.

*

I am no longer a visitor in this country and yet I still feel wonder at America's inexhaustible roads. Their patterns comfort me. I thrill at repetition, like a baby who squeals at the third iteration of a gesture, as if learning the joke of the world. I know now that a cluster of firework stores heralds a state boundary and that up in the mountains the radio pop songs will all burst into Jesus by the chorus. Even the arrangements that disturb me – the confederate flags, which multiply or dwindle depending on whether we're heading south or north from Virginia – feel grounding in my ability to predict them. We passed billboard promises – *Christ Saves* – *Table dancing! Fully nude!* Above us, injury lawyers beamed down in benediction upon the highway – *When you are hurt, we will come to you.* Through the mining towns the radio asked, *Have you been affected by black lung?* I was struck, as I often am, by this country's breadth and mystery and my uncanny sense of having seen it all before, place names unspooling along the highway, like the lyrics to a half-remembered song.

At dusk we reached our destination, coming off the highway onto *Hell for Certain Road.* Our path was lined by daisies and orange day lilies, their naked stalks thrust out towards the track, and a contraceptive apothecary of thistles and Queen Anne's lace. I counted seven rabbits, streaking out at intervals, their skinny back legs in quick motion as they darted away beneath our headlights along *Devil's Jump Branch.* The forbiddingly named roads narrowed and twisted through steep woodland. My whole body engaged as we attempted, in our tiny car, to climb and descend the slopes. On the final hill, we halted and began to slide backwards. *Come on, come on*, I whispered to the car, and I was proud of it as it struggled up once more. As we finally rolled down into the *holler*, an Appalachian word, derived from *hollow*, denoting a valley between mountains, at six miles an hour, I felt that we had passed into a different world, scooped out from the ordinary one, life and the pandemic held back by the woods and the highway. The fireflies were coming out, and there was our friend Christine, walking up the track to greet us.

It was a calculated risk to meet her here, in this patch of rural Kentucky, a rough midpoint between our home in Virginia and hers in Chicago, a place none of us had anything to do with. I had taken a Covid test – a nurse in Mickey Mouse Crocs had slid a swab deeper into my nostril than I thought possible – and so had Christine, and we had chosen the spot for its remoteness from strangers. And yet I felt guilt at hugging her. I also felt sheer joy at her small frame in my arms, at being close enough to smell her hair, her softness and warmth, like an apricot, joy at hugging someone other than Luke, a woman, a creature of my own dimensions. And during our days at the campsite – a field behind an isolated house with woods rising all around – it was a gift to be domestic with someone else, to watch Christine's graceful hands as she made salad for the three of us at a table outside, her fingers raking through lettuce leaves and dropping them into a bowl, withdrawing long, pale radishes from a bag and carefully slicing them, the silver flash of her knife.

In the holler, the quiet was full of sound, insects and whippoorwills calling the sharp, instant syllables of their own names. June bugs lay buzzing in the grass at our feet, too heavy to fly, and we discovered dozens of orange fritillary butterflies congregating on a slip of mud to feast on its salts. We walked to a lake, swam and came back sunburnt. We made fires and read *The Arabian Nights* by the light of our headlamps.

And just beyond the boundary of this place the world was more broken than I had ever known it. Touch had fallen from our lives. We did not trust the police or the president. A friend had been so ill that she could not walk for months, even though Covid was supposed to harm our age group only briefly on its path through our bodies to more vulnerable ones.

I had written to my grandfather, *Have you ever lived through a moment that felt anything like this?* and wondered if he'd reply that it was akin to his wartime childhood. Or perhaps, I had thought, he might tell me something instructive about what it was like to live with the fear of nuclear war, and to decide, even then, to have children. But he had ignored my question and replied with a description of his garden, where I had picked and eaten sour apples as a little girl. Sitting on the grass in Kentucky, I watched a garter snake swallow a toad and I wrote Grandad a long description of the snake's body draped along the verge, the toad's flailing front legs, and how it eventually became a lump under the snake's skin.

We weren't all alone in the holler, though it mostly felt like it. Our host was a woman of indeterminate old age who went by Yaya. She walked down to the field masked and barefoot to greet us after feeding her chickens and said she didn't mind the pandemic because she never left her holler. I could imagine her coming up out of the ground here, born an old woman lying on her side beneath a patch of black-eyed Susans. There was a collective global effort taking place on Saturday night, she told us, to call aliens to Earth. That's the night of the lunar eclipse, we said, but she didn't know anything about that. When we asked why we would want to call aliens to Earth she smiled, like it was obvious, and said, *To help us.*

A man appeared down by the lake. He stepped forward to Luke and tugged at his lower eyelid, revealing the red of it, fleshy, almost genital, to ask, *Hey, can you see a bug in my eye?* Luke looked carefully but said no. It was the closest he had been to a stranger in months. We were surprised by a chain of quadbikes speeding through the woods, confederate flags rippling from their thin roofs. Christine was shocked by them, though we were not, but only because we lived in Virginia and she in Chicago.

While Christine was washing in Yaya's solar shower, with its tangle of black hoses like a nest of eels, I carefully tweezered ticks from Luke's legs. We deposited their tiny apple-seed bodies in zip-lock bags in case they needed to be tested later for Lyme disease. It was the fourth of July. Luke told me he had been worrying about a right-wing revolution on this date. We speculated about how we would know, upon leaving the holler, that it had happened. Roadblocks, perhaps, being met at the mouth of the highway by drawn weapons. His face clouded and he said, *I've encountered these people, so I take them seriously.* His voice was soft among the bird calls.

Three summers before he had stood in the crowd in Charlottesville that the car had ploughed into, killing a young woman. That was the year before we met. I once saw a press photo of that moment, in which he was visible, my future husband, frozen forever in the instant of diving away.

By the fire that night Christine asked Luke when he had stopped loving her. She asked indirectly, saying, *I sometimes want to ask you . . .*, making it more cerebral than emotional, a conversation about the desire to ask. She and I sat on low camping chairs almost facing but angled towards the fire. Luke sat between us on a mat, cross-legged like a child. Fires draw things out of us. They give us something to look at when we speak, besides one another. It was dark, and I could only see their figures, not their faces. I did not like the conversation, which pulled us all back into a time when my partner was Christine's partner, a time before I existed for either of them. But I knew about that past, and even admired it, the abandon with which they fell in love. I knew also that the future they once imagined together had not come, that it was Luke and I who were married, and that Christine was married too, to somebody else. Yet I hardened for a moment against the rawness of her heart. We listened to the quiet and then to an unknown animal screaming its want through the woods behind us, calling and calling into the darkness for a mate. Then Luke rose and poured water from a plastic bowl onto the embers of the fire so we could go to bed, and they died with a brief plume of smoke.

When I met Luke, I experienced a profound intuition to be near him. Then a friend told me his sister had just died, and I thought, *Yes, I know something about that.* Not long afterwards we went together to a vigil and protest on the first anniversary of the Charlottesville attack. It was very hot, and I was wearing a linen top that left part of my back bare, which I was embarrassed by because everyone else had come in boots and bandanas, the uniform of those ready to be tear-gassed. At one point, Luke laid a hand on my back to make sure we did not separate in the crowd. The quick feeling of his palm against my skin. It was the first time he ever touched me.

That summer of 2020, I felt our marriage to be a space scooped out of this world, an enclosure of quiet. A hollow space requires negation, wishes unfulfilled, loves that didn't work out. And a hollow negates; because I was here, vacationing in the middle of nowhere, Kentucky – noticing rat droppings in the sawdust of the long-drop toilet, admiring the beauty of Yaya's chickens as their feathers glowed in the day's last light, being loved and having my hand taken by Luke with such care as we made our way through the woods – I was not in England. I knew how quickly life could change and people could be lost, that I had already been away longer than the period of time between my brother's diagnosis and his death. But there is no life without loss, without danger. They had entered our lives in large and small ways, and now flinted at the edges in the shapes of disease and unspeakable violence. The questions had to be, what space does loss carve out? What can be built there?

The sky was shrouded in cloud on our final night, concealing the lunar eclipse. We burnt our remaining wood and read *The Arabian Nights*. A demon granted a fisherman a series of increasingly ludicrous wishes. Green bugs flew into our foreheads, drawn by the beams of our headlamps. Not long before, when the world was its recognisable self, I had gone to a festival in Michigan with Luke and Christine. Walking around the lake, through groups of people and so many scattered twinkling lights, we came upon a giant magic lamp. There was a door in its side, just big enough for us to crawl through, revealing that the belly of the lamp was a little room. Inside was a genie. And although the genie was just a bald man, smiling in silly blue robes, and his enormous lamp only painted plywood, I felt a child-like seriousness when he asked for my wish. The night outside the lamp was cool and lovely, reflected fires shimmering on the lake. I told the genie that I wished to continue my life. *That's it?* he said. But he granted it anyway, and ever since it had been coming true.

In the morning we slid the poles from our tents and folded them away, before perching by the cold ashes of our fire to write letters to Yaya's aliens. It seemed unlikely that the aliens would be real and literate and in the business of granting wishes, yet we asked for audacious things like the strength to accept the chaos of the world. We asked for children. We returned the huge round folding table Yaya had lent us, rolling it across the property on its side like a giant wheel. As we drove out, she yelled, *I'm your new redneck Kentucky granny*. I wondered what her version of summoning the aliens had looked like, alone in her ramshackle house by the field.

For a while we moved slowly through the woods in convoy, Christine's car ahead of us because it had front-wheel drive so would not slide backwards on the steep tracks. I imagined those front wheels gripping the slopes like claws. Then the road split around a croft of bluestem grass. It was green at the bottom, fading to feathery yellow as it rose, the kind of grass that beckons to be stroked, a soft harbour for ticks. Christine rolled down her window to call back at us before we diverged, the grass so tall it almost obscured her car, its red top just visible as she slid away. I sometimes think that she and I will live together, one day long from now, two old ladies with a garden of yellow flowers, after Luke is dead. Before we hit the highway, I saw a huge owl, perched in a tree by the road. A sort of verbose inarticulacy overtakes me at moments like this and I could not manage to say, *Look*, but only, *Great big beautiful owl!* as it took flight from its branch, revealing the bright white undersides of its wings. It landed deeper in the woods, still watching us.

And then we met the main road. There was no roadblock, just the smooth asphalt and a twangy voice on the radio singing, *What you gonna do with my old tattoo? How you gonna hide my name?* After the song, a bulletin jolted us back to the pandemic: there had been almost three million cases now in the US alone. I spoke little, feeling like a fissure of quiet had broken open within me and the rest of myself was rushing into it. We were returning home to our carrot seedlings and our intimate loneliness, the gnawing fear of catching Covid, of passing it to someone it could kill. *Get Saved or the Devil Will Get You*, a billboard warned. By the turn-off for Hungry Mother State Park, a sign thanked *God and veterans for our independence.* And then came the firework stores, the boundary between states.

Not long in the future, I would hold the small clutch of letters Granddad had sent over the pandemic, each of which ended, *I look forward to meeting your new husband*, and they would be all I had of him in the world. He would die before I had the chance to see him again or to introduce them. In the future, the right-wing uprising Luke had feared would come to pass, or at least it would seem like it for a day. I would call him, out for a rare trip into the world on his own, and tell him, with a tremor in my voice, what I was seeing on the news. He'd rush back to our kitchen table to watch CNN with me in horror: the repeating clips of the Capitol being stormed, the same window smashing over and over again. In the future, a woman from the FBI would call Luke to tell him he had been doxed as suspected Antifa, his name and our address revealed on a right-wing website, and we'd file this alongside the rest of the news, alarming but somehow also remote, hard to work out a response to. My green card would arrive. We would walk into a disused JCPenney department store still decked with posters of laughing women in long-dead fashions to receive our vaccines – administered by members of the National Guard, polite and handsome as action dolls in their uniforms. And we would wait to see if we'd been gifted or cursed by Yaya's aliens.

That day in 2020, we drove until our bodies ached. As we came into Virginia, lightning flashed above the road, each fork clear, as if drawn in silver pen. There is a particular smell in Virginia, a sort of vegetable sweetness, when rain comes smashing through the summer heat. I felt the pull of *home*, our little house in Charlottesville a magnet, its charge strengthening the closer we grew to it. When the rain stopped, an abrupt calm fell. I remembered walking through a storm ten years before in a long red dress, holding a former beloved's hand. We had entered a restaurant soaked through and I'd dripped red dye across the floor as we found a table, a trail behind me of everywhere I had been.

Look, Luke said, breaking my daydream. There was pink shining through a tear in the sky and the edges of the clouds were gilded with light. He is so good at alerting me to beauty. All the loveliness in this world I might have missed.

Where Lost Things Go

We meet Scott, an ex-military diver we found on the internet, in the parking lot at Roaring Run. It's the summer of 2021 and the morning is unseasonably cool for Virginia in July. He shakes our hands, instantly talkative, with that same eager confidence he'd had on the phone when he'd told us, *Gold is twenty-five times heavier than water*, and, *Now, this isn't a political thing, but I will be carrying a firearm.* I look but don't see the shape of one as he gathers gear from his truck into a black holdall, which he shoulders before hoisting on his oxygen tank and metal detector. Together we make our way to the mouth of the trail. The trees and vines are fuller than when Luke and I came here last, each leaf holding the light like a piece of stained glass.

We last came to this place six weeks before with one of Luke's eight sisters and her family. The trail leads up to Roaring Run Falls, a waterfall split around a huge rock. Along the way lie smaller falls and swimming holes, each of them a discreet world. We had stopped that day at a pool with a sheet of red rock sloping into it, forming a natural waterslide. There was something about the place – the way the rush of the river was gathered by the pool, which held it a while, almost still: it seemed outside of normal time. Watching Luke in the water, I thought about what a boy he was, though he is older than me and older than he looks. He splashed in, yelping at the cold, laughing with the sun on his shoulders, diving down briefly, then coming up with his fringe flat to his face. There are few pleasures like watching someone you love in a state of unselfconscious happiness. We had spent most of our marriage alone due to the pandemic, and it was still wondrous to be among others, our nephew testing the water with his feet, my sister-in-law undaunted by the cold, brave in her black swimming costume. The branches above patterned everything with shadow. After a while, we dried off and resumed our ascent to the falls.

Then, not far up the trail, Luke looked at his left hand and found that his wedding ring had vanished.

I scrambled after him as he ran back down the path and climbed over the rocks and into the water, still in his clothes and shoes. He began to look, swiping through the water skaters and floating leaves. Of course, it was useless. The water was too murky, the area too large. I put my arms around him in the shallows of the pool, water up to our knees. I could feel the commotion in his body, all heat and freshwater chill, the way adrenaline surges and drains when there's nothing at all to be done.

It doesn't matter, I said, *it doesn't matter.*

*

Objects allow us to decant some of the meaning in our lives, so we don't have to hold it all within us every second. And objects make meanings lighter to bear – so light they might even slip off and sink through cold water when our fingers pale and shrink.

But objects do not matter. Not really. I know this for sure.

The ring was titanium lined in gold with an inscription inside, handmade for us. Luke looked desolate as we walked on to the falls and down through a different part of the woods, the tan line on his finger a photonegative of the ring. That night, he rolled towards me in bed, his face full of worry.

Do you think it's a bad omen?

Shocked at his superstition, I firmly said, *No*.

And yet, I couldn't help but imagine opening my palm and offering it back to him, the magic trick it would be if we could somehow find it.

Of all the outlandish questions I have hurled into Google, *Lost wedding ring what to do?* turned out to be one of the few with a practical answer. I was taken to a site with a map of the United States, dotted with the locations of ring finders. And there was Scott, not far from us, with the symbol of a tiny diver in silhouette beside his name.

*

Through the woods Scott talks about the Marines, how he dived beside trained sea lions and dolphins with spears on their noses, and about the job he was offered in New York City's sewer system, which he declined even though it was 600 grand a year. *They give you a ton of vaccines*, he told us. *In the suit, you can't smell anything.* We edge slowly up the trail because his equipment is so heavy. His stories concerning rings have a fairy-tale quality. Once he grasped what felt like a ring underwater, but it turned out to be a shell with a perfect circular hole through it. As he lifted it into the beam of his lamp it was stolen by a catfish. Once he searched and searched for a ring only for it to turn up beneath the lady's pillow. In huge, dark lakes, you don't even try to see, he tells us; you put down a line of carabiners and pull yourself along it, slowly, with your eyes closed.

The pool appears below us, as lovely as the day we found it. Luke and I perch on rocks while Scott prepares to dive, pulling his wetsuit on over his tattooed back. Luke goes down to help him when the zip catches. Tiny things crawl over my legs, though they are sticky with bug spray. A group of Mennonite women with hair coverings, surrounded by little kids, pause to peer down at Scott standing in full diving gear, readying his metal detector. It is amazing to me that this device will be able to trace an object as small as a ring, casting out electromagnetic waves and turning them into sound. If Scott does find it, it will be by listening.

All right, he says, then vanishes. We can track where he is by the silver shape of his oxygen tank breaking the surface or bubbles rising in succession, the occasional flash of his headlamp.

Five years before, I lost several objects in a single moment. When I discovered they had vanished, I also lost my mind.

I use the word *lost* deliberately, though at the time my mind instead felt broken, cleanly and quickly snapped, like a pencil or a bone. It was September 2016, a warm evening in Central London. Before the incident, I'd sat in a red vinyl booth in the bar of Soho Theatre with my friend Danny, our hands resting on the particleboard table. *I just really need nothing else to happen. I'm on the edge*, I said, with the irony demanded of the pat phrase. We laughed. We did not know that a few hours later I would be screaming in the street.

I have only ever been robbed while weak in some way, and the months leading up to that night had weakened me. First came an ordinary wound: on a spring Sunday on Streatham Common, I broke up with a man I still loved. When we rose from the discussion, little pieces of grass clung to our clothes. It was the right thing to do, but it was also the end of a flare of magic in my life. I'd met him a few years into bereavement and falling in love had felt like opening a door in the shadowy house of myself and finding an unknown room full of light. But my love was only ever vaguely requited. Deciding to leave was good for my dignity, but hard on my brain, which flooded with foolish chemical delight in his presence, oxytocin-tenderness.

John had now been dead three and a half years. And I had finally stopped seeing fragility everywhere, stopped imagining friends' organs under their skins. I'd become more like a real young person, who could go to parties and dance in a staticky dress like life was everlasting. But that spring, a close friend became suicidal. I wrapped him in an apron in my kitchen, and we made bread, flour falling softly into the bowl, the dough growing strong and elastic under the heels of our hands: anything to keep him distracted and under my eye. I felt afraid and limited, angry that death would dare to come near me again so soon.

Then in June, I received a call from my dad while walking across a field and I knew something awful had happened, though his voice was very light. When I went over to my parents' house, he told me and Max that our mum had ovarian cancer, while she picked herbs outside, singing 'Jolene'. I remember looking at Max's face, the U-shaped scar on their cheek where they had once been bitten by a miniature circus horse. It could be swiftly dealt with, our dad said. It wouldn't be like John's cancer, which had killed him within a year of diagnosis. There would be no need for chemotherapy or to be unduly worried.

On the morning of her surgery, I woke in an improvised bed made of two sofas pushed together into a sort of cot, miles away from her at the Edinburgh Festival where I was working. Half dreaming, I pictured my mum, small enough to lie down on her side in the palm of my hand, offering her with an outstretched arm to the care of the NHS. I wanted to fly back to London, but my dad told me not to, that there would be plenty of time in the coming months to be with her as she recovered. And so, I carried on working and having the kind of apocalypse good time that the festival demands, sleeping just a few hours each night. It was as if the fear I had experienced during John's illness had clawed a space for itself within me, which it returned to now, nesting like an animal, snug and almost quiet. When I eventually saw my mum, she had the imploded look of a person who had had six body parts removed. *Touch my tummy*, she said, and it felt jelly-like, fragile, as if a wall had been removed and replaced by a curtain. We laughed together at the scar running from her breastbone down into her leggings. It wriggled over her skin, raised and red, like a worm held down with surgical staples. *You'd have thought they'd have bloody well sewn it straight*, she said. The operation had been a great success.

Looking back at this chain of non-disasters, from which all parties emerged bruised but alive, I now see loss. Of love, all its comforts and gestures; that musty bedroom in Streatham no longer mine to lie down in against a naked back, no one to call late at night when bad things happened. Loss of my unspoken arrangement with death; I had thought it would keep away from me a while, but then came the fragility of my friend's neck, and a return to the world of hospitals and sterile yellow bins in the living room for the disposing of needles. Little losses, against the vast loss of John. I worked a lot at this time and dated and did complicated things with my hair. On the outside, I think I seemed very confident. But I had begun to feel lost inside my life.

By that September, I was overcaffeinated and under-slept, which is also part of what happened to my mind.

That evening in Soho, Danny and I and our other house-mates went to see a play. I have no idea what it was; it has been completely wiped from my memory. Afterwards we sat together in a pizza place beside the theatre. It was dark in there, a flame flickering in a cup of clear oil on our table. I remember laughing and the cold sweetness of a cocktail, the feeling of my shoulders relaxing into my back. Then we got up to leave, and I reached under the table for my bag and discovered that it was gone.

I had been carrying four notebooks. One of my own, and three written by John, chronicling the final year of his life. His handwriting was very small and irregular but careful. So much of him seemed carried in the shapes of his letters and occasional misspellings. They were a portal back to him. I had them with me that day because they made me feel safe. I thought John, alive inside those pages in the movements of his thoughts, might somehow tell me what to do next with my life.

*

Here is what had happened. Days later, a kind woman from the restaurant, whose name was also Anna, described the CCTV footage to me over the phone. Two thieves, either a couple, or posing as a couple, had sat at the next table, pretending to be ordinary customers like the rest of us. At some point, the man slid my bag from under my seat with his foot (I had not done my usual practice in busy places of winding a strap around my leg). The woman took it, slipped it onto her shoulder and the pair walked out into the street. An elegant act.

Panic rushed through me. I scrabbled under the table, pulling back all our seats. I searched the floor around us, interrupting people's conversations, my face flushed with sweat, then I ran upstairs to search the toilets, though I knew it wasn't there, and then out into the street where I screamed, *No*, and some sounds that were not words. Someone brought me a chair; it arrived under me out on the pavement. It was night, Soho a blur of voices and lights. My sweat cooled and I began to shiver. The world and my limbs and the folds of my brain seemed to swell and congeal. And yet, a few things appeared strangely sharp: the yellow painted line on the pavement, the way it broke and continued around a drain, and my clear sense of having lost my place in the world, as if reality had expelled me and I was supposed to be dead.

At home, I found myself frightened to be by myself in my bedroom, so Danny lay beside me on top of the covers until my heart slowed. My bed was beneath a window backing onto the station. After he slipped out, I lay listening to the metal roar of passing trains for hours. I felt like an animal when I woke, a creature from the tangled bank between our back fence and the tracks, with burrs in its fur and a stinking mouth and no business being in the house. In the backyard, I stood beneath the elder that twisted up from the concrete and called my mum, weeping, ashamed of what had happened.

Come here, she said. *It doesn't matter, it doesn't matter.* After that I stayed with my parents for weeks. My voice slid from my body, and I cried all the time, as if some staunching mechanism in me had simply been removed. I called off work and dwelled obsessively on the lost notebooks. Thoughts swam through me, dark and slickly dangerous, violent images that made me conscious of my breakable skin.

There is a temptation to weigh circumstance against reaction when reviewing mental crises. To think, *That's it? That's what made you lose your mind?* I sometimes feel that these events were not enough, as if one could be ill-qualified for a breakdown. But I have known several people who have *lost it*, and their reaction has rarely matched their apparent circumstances. One might bear a bereavement but go to pieces over a vanished pet, that little bird who flew out into winter, taking forever his tropical trilling voice and orange cheeks, his lungs the size of a thumbnail. One might fall apart in the safe arms of a quiet summer, decades after an act of violence.

I discovered an instinct, a tiny intact part of myself, glinting like a scrunch of tinfoil on the ground. I was exhausted, but the instinct said, *Stillness will kill you*, and so each day, I forced myself to walk past the gardens and painted front doors to the post box at the end of my parents' road. I have never before or since found an activity as gruelling as those brief walks, when the world seemed to warp around me, that red post box stretching further and further away. But the instinct had a kind of authority over me, for which I will always be grateful.

One morning when the post box seemed too far, my dad persuaded me into the car and drove us out to a lake in Kent. I could hardly move or speak and lay flat on the backseat all the way. *Just try to get in for a few minutes*, he said when we arrived, and somehow I pulled on my wetsuit – friction from the neoprene against my skin – and bundled my hair into a latex hat. He zipped me up. I had been to this place when I was well. I'd taken a test where I swam along with a man watching me from a boat and had been awarded a laminated card afterwards: this person is safe here, this person is strong. There were divers at the water's edge, loading on gear, ready to make their way to places I'd never see. I'd heard there was a double-decker bus somewhere in the depths, like something from a legend. I walked barefoot down the concrete slope.

And then the water took me, first by my naked feet and then my whole suited body, my bare hands, my face. There was a moment before the chill found its way under my hat and reached the follicles of my scalp. My blood vessels flew open and then drew tight to guard my heart. I swam, making a path around the edge of the lake with the rolling crawl my dad had taught me. Energy poured out of me, keeping me in motion through the cold. Soft winds blew over the water's surface, making planes of movement, not quite waves. Every three strokes, I tilted my head to gulp from the sky. Grey blue over me and all around me green, a world of light and drifting particles, my white fingers and each black-clad arm sliding past my ear, along my cheek, then out in front, before pulling back against the water, propelling me on. Occasionally, a diver deep below would split open a seam of cold, which would rush up to meet me like a ghost. I swam for a long time, far longer than I'd thought I could.

After I got out, I stood on the bank in a huge, insulated coat, my fingers prickling back to life around a polystyrene cup of sweet tea, watching my dad complete a few more laps. I thought of the broken rib that had pierced the soft flesh of his left lung in an accident some years before. He had brought me here to this place, which would hold me, as a way of loving me without words. Nearby, a group of women shared a tin of cake. Too tough for wetsuits, they laughed together in their bright swimming costumes and flowered swimming hats. I finished my tea as my dad came out shivering. Sunshine broke over the deck, and

I briefly let its warmth reclaim me. He pointed out one of the group, smiling in her crisscross-back swimming costume, and as we drove away, he told me that she held the record for the slowest swim ever across the English Channel. Thirty-six hours: so much more impressive than the fastest crossing. *Imagine*, he said, *keeping going like that, hour after hour, in all that cold.*

That autumn, I began work on a community project at Battersea Arts Centre, a creative response to the fire that had destroyed the oldest section of the building the year before. When the producer called to set the project in motion, I did not tell her that I had lost my mind since she'd hired me that summer, that I saw no one and had left my adult life to spend my days watching television with my mum, rising only to make tea or to inject blood thinner into her stomach. I said I'd come in that Tuesday.

And I found that I could get up in front of groups of strangers – school children and older Battersea residents – and ask them to write stories and poems. I could sit with the patient young archivist and look at fragile paper programmes, vestiges of the dances, plays and rallies the building had held before it vanished into flames. I spent the rest of my hours crying on trains or imagining a stranger sliding a knife between my ribs. We needed to recruit more elderly people for the project, so I went to a tea dance and spent the afternoon waltzing clumsily around a hall with elegant old men and women, trusting myself to the confidence of their wrinkled hands. But at my own grandparents' wedding anniversary, I could barely speak to anyone or process the sounds coming from my relatives' mouths. In the group photograph my face is unsmiling, strained, the face of a person with something wrong with them.

One day, a friend who did not know what had happened invited me to meet up. I hesitated: what if I went only to blink at him slowly, unable to speak? But I knew he had been depressed in the past, which made me feel safer. And then there I was, by the Thames, drinking coffee, the two of us talking by the river's rough light, our discussion a little fire in the autumn air. Another piece of myself, mundane but remarkable to me, momentarily refound.

When I managed to go home, my bedroom in the house I shared with Danny and my other friends seemed quiet from its time without me. I discovered an archive among my things. I kept two well-ordered bookcases, but only a single shelf was my own; the rest was filled with John's second-hand Penguin Classics, the pages yellowed and the print small. His camera sat on my dresser and in the wardrobe were his best warm jumper and his blue duffle coat with its plastic ivory toggles. John had in fact once lived in this house with the twisting elder in the backyard. I had thought that by staying here, in this city and this light-blue bedroom, by keeping John's possessions so carefully, I could somehow carry his life into the future alongside my own.

But the responsibility was too great. The theft had made a joke of my plan.

John Berger writes, 'What I did not know when I was very young was that nothing can take the past away: the past grows gradually around one, like a placenta for dying.'

I had tried to protect the past, clinging to it tightly and staying as still as I could. But what if it could travel with me, nourishing me quietly, even as it fell away?

Up swam a question: how exactly did I want to live?

I had committed far in advance to working as a drama-turge on a one-man show in Iceland, and so I went and sat in the corner of the rehearsal room, quietly writing down notes to discuss with the playwright. In Reykjavik the bathwater smelt softly and not unpleasantly of eggs. Our rehearsal room had a poster on the wall, which read, *What is the best that could happen?* A fridge-magnet phrase, which I found caustically poignant. All week in Iceland, I lay in the liminal space between sleep and waking, reading John's notebooks in my mind. His gratitude to our dad for not hugging him at hospital after his diagnosis – *he knew how much it would scare me.* The incantation near the end, *I shall fill my lungs with air and return home.* I discovered pages and pages almost intact in me. I had thought of him as encoded in the books, as a tree is encoded in a walnut. But he was encoded in me also.

In that stark, unfamiliar country, I could hold my past in a looser grip. And the less tightly I held, the more of it returned.

I visited Thingvellir National Park, where the earth lies ripped open by shifting tectonic plates, cliffs of solidified lava lining that long tear in the ground.

Where do lost things go? Where is the great rift in the world they fall into, or might be unearthed from?

Back in London, in a room high above the street at London Bridge, I went to therapy. This is where I truly refound my mind, pink and quivering as a newborn mouse. When my bones fizzled with sadness, I would walk all the way there from my home in Croydon, passing the Maudsley en route where a friend of mine had briefly lived while sectioned. There was comfort in the knowledge that if I just kept going step by step over the pavements, I would arrive at the therapist's office in a handful of hours.

Winter came and I stood in a long line at Battersea post office holding a brown Manila envelope containing forty pages of my writing. I sent it to a graduate programme in the United States because I wanted to reach out to something far beyond my life.

The year turned.
    Dark thoughts still came, but differently.
    I completed my project about the Battersea Arts Centre fire. A commander from the fire brigade told me, *It sounds bad, but we live for fires like this*, and gave me a series of thermal images of the blaze. My collaborator, a designer

and dear friend, made light boxes from the pictures, and for the final exhibition we embedded the voice recordings of the witnesses I had interviewed into them, cut-together stories pouring softly from that burning place.

It was spring, shreds of cut grass in the parks, and I was almost ordinary again, by which I mean that the world at last felt real. It had stopped warping around me. I had stopped picturing sharp objects and sudden harms. And happiness, minutes and days of it, sometimes came back for me.

Yet I had the peculiar sensation that London – the city that had seemed to open up further and further before me in the eleven years I'd lived there – had closed. Reality had readmitted me. I was supposed to be alive, just somewhere else. And then I got an email from the graduate programme in Virginia, offering me a fully funded place to study on the other side of the Atlantic.

As I knelt on the floor in my bedroom by the train tracks, everything I owned lay around me. Aside from my collection of John's things were an overwhelming number of possessions of my own. Every card or note I'd ever received was sheathed in cardboard under my bed, beside the pink silk dance shoes with blocks in the toes, which I hadn't worn in a decade, and thick folders of highlighted notes from my A-levels. There was the copper-brown synthetic dress I had discarded so often on the floor of a Streatham bedroom, charged with remembered tenderness. And the green cotton dress I had once worn while rowing in Crystal Palace Park with John and our dad – surely, if I could just slide into it, I would be back inside that lost afternoon, moving steadily over the lake.

The word clutter comes from *clot*, that faithful mechanism that stops us bleeding and can also cause great harm. It took me days to pack it all up into bags for the bin and the charity shop. I then packed John's things with care and, because they did not only belong to me but to all my family, sent them to rest in my parents' attic. The room's new emptiness exposed it. I had painted it badly, but it was full of light.

I no longer had John's books. But I possessed still his desire to pass them to me, my acceptance of that request. Our sincerity was intact.

I moved to America with a single silver suitcase. My mum bought it, moving slowly around TK Maxx, although she had technically now recovered. She was infinitely patient that day as I examined each case one by one. I remembered the panicked gratitude that had engulfed me back in September, when I'd arrived at her house newly out of my mind. How I'd sat beside her on the stairs, held her small body and sobbed, *I am so glad you are alive.*

It is hard to love people and to walk away from them through an airport, knowing how fragile we all are. But shrinking one's life, moulding it like protective foam around all that is breakable, does not work. Loss is coming either way. And my instinct, which had once warned, *Stillness will kill you*, now said simply, *Move forward*.

I loved that silver suitcase: striding out into JFK Airport with it, its material link with my mum. But later, when it buckled from too many books and became home to the bedbugs nesting in my Virginia bedroom, I let it go.

When John was dying, his life falling away from him like gold through water, he wrote the following in his neat but rebellious hand: *I hope to keep thinking clearly and to write what I think.* For a while, I wanted to engrave those words on the inside of a bracelet, to wear them in silver against my pulse. But I never committed to doing so, despite enquiring at many jewellers. Creating another object that contained a trace of his voice perhaps just felt too dangerous. Besides, the phrase was engraved already on the inside of my mind.

To keep thinking clearly and to write what I think: it is also what I hope for.

And when things fall apart, and I can't think or write down anything, I hope to be taken swimming, to rest my body into something more fluid than my mind, something that flows around what happens to it and never stops moving.

We wait on a rock by the pool at Roaring Run. With a fingertip, I trace the rough, curled edges of lichen blooms.

Scott bobs up briefly to show us a lump of stone laced with pyrite, which had set off the detector. My heart jumps a bit each time we see him pause a while in a single spot, and yet I'm struck by how little it really matters whether or not the ring is found.

The evening after we lost it, we went to a party at my old house. Excited to be out after the long confinement of the pandemic, I put on an excess of sparkly blue eyeshadow, then spent much of the night explaining that I didn't usually look like this. The kitchen was full of poets and without fail each said, *At least you lost it in a beautiful place*, when we told them about the ring. Later we laughed, *Damn poets*. But it was true that we could shape the meaning of the loss, decide something, just as we had agreed that the loop of titanium lined with gold meant that we were married.

Our first date had been at a swimming hole with a waterfall flowing into it. We'd walked back in silence, hoping to see animals emerge as dusk fell, and even though the bears kept to themselves, a presence did appear between us as we made our way back to Luke's car with dripping hair, our future togetherness already looming into being. Then there was the time at another waterfall when we had stripped naked and jumped in, only to be surprised by a party of thirty geology students. The poem I associate most with my husband, who often pulls off his shoes and socks whenever we cross a creek and kicks his legs in delight when his feet meet the cold, is Raymond Carver's 'Where Water Comes Together with Other

Water'. If the ring had to be lost, what better place for it than here?

A ring is a thing, and things do not matter. Not when we've been down to the silt of ourselves. And yet, it is miraculous when Scott breaks the surface with something small and circular pinched between his finger and thumb: a magician's reveal. We rush down to the water and confirm that, yes, it is ours, titanium lined with gold, inscribed on the inside. We take photographs, Luke smiling and holding up his hand, the ring, just slightly tarnished, back upon his finger. I touch it, and it feels imbued with cold. We walk slowly with Scott back down to the cars, and he tells us more stories. It was love at first sight with his wife. He's a direct descendant of Mary, Queen of Scots. And then he vanishes in his white Ford pick-up to his other job, running a gun range, and we stay and walk up to the falls.

Later he messages, *Thank you for trusting me with your ring*.

The bottom of the pool was rocky and dark, Scott told us, littered with little gromets from people's swimsuits and dozens of lost acrylic nails. But I picture this: the hairpin I found at thirteen in a box of my dead grandmother's possessions, which I kept in my pocket until the day I carelessly left it in a friend's car and was too shy to explain that such an ordinary object mattered to me; the white plastic watch I bought at an airport with the solemn yet broken promise to myself never to misplace it; the banknotes pressed into a Christmas card, which I accidentally threw away; the metal straw I left in the seatback of an aeroplane; John's books, their ink dissolving, filling the water with voice. Everything I have ever lost gathered below the pool's shifting surface, out of sight but safe. Just beyond the reach of my hands.

Part 3

—

Home

Home

Unlikely but possible etymology from Welsh *cu* (*'beloved, dear'*)

How to Live Without Your Brother

Lee's email came at dusk as I left a yoga class, the muscles soft along the backs of my legs. We had been at university together and seen each other just a handful of times in the years since. He came over once for dinner at my house near Croydon and we had made flatbreads at my little square table, stretching the dough in our hands, flour thickening the air. As I washed up afterwards, my then boyfriend accused me of flirting with Lee, which I was in a sexless sort of way – if flirting is to turn the lamp of your attention on another person. I admired his poems.

Another time, he had invited me to a party at a restaurant in Covent Garden. His brother was there. The two of them looked quite different but shared a certain clear-skinned attractiveness borne of workouts and self-denial. They had the kind of bodies that seemed unmarked by life. At university, Lee sometimes spoke about *the Philosophy of the CrossFit Movement*. He'd shake his head when I brought coffee into class: *I just don't know how you can put that in your body*. At the restaurant, we all sat at a long table. The brother and I were at opposite ends, so I never spoke to him. I had a drink with a strawberry in it.

Carbon bubbles rose in my glass and clung to its red sides before breaking. Lee and I both got things wrong that evening. I had bought his girlfriend, who was leaving the country, a birthday card because I had somehow got confused about what the party was for. *It's nice*, Lee said, *much less sad than her going away.* He stood and thanked us all for coming, then made some small joke at his brother's expense and his brother became cross and left early.

Now, I read Lee's words in the street. His brother was dead.

When you are very young and a death explodes your life, you can feel peerless. After John died, during my second year at university, Lee stopped me on the stairs to offer condolences and I began to weep. He put his hands out, embarrassed, and said, *I'm sorry, I'm sorry, I shouldn't have brought it up.* He seemed annoyed at himself, but also a little annoyed at me. Six years had elapsed between that moment and his email appearing on my phone. *It's really hard*, he wrote, *every day it all evolves.* Then came the question, framed as a cautious statement: *Maybe you know how to make it easier?*

There was so much hope couched in his syntax. Had he asked directly, *Do you know how to make it easier?* I might have answered directly. I might have said, *No.*

A few years later, after I became a lecturer, a student called Hannah stayed behind in my classroom, her arms wrapped around her waist, after everyone else had left.

She told me that just before she came to college her brother had died. I was teaching a mandatory course for first-year students, aimed at helping them write academic essays. As a writer of plays and fiction, I felt vaguely fraudulent in my role, ever poised for a question about grammar that I couldn't address. Hannah was an excellent writer, though she didn't think of herself that way. Her sentences flowed like thought and I had tried to explain to her that not everyone could do that. She was funny and outgoing in class, and yet, when she told me of this enormous sadness, I found myself unsurprised. I recognised in her, I think, some of the caution with which I had moved through most of my undergraduate degree – wary of others, carrying death like a substance liable to spill.

That semester, she wrote a beautiful essay about prayer as a somatic practice for bearing grief. One by one her peers, so very young and so very American, offered the feedback that she should make it more positive. This began an email exchange between us, which has lasted for years. Her first subject line was: *Peer feedback sucks*. Variations on the same class were offered by at least forty different instructors; she might have ended up being taught by any of them. She might have taken the class with someone who could answer grammar questions without pausing for breath. But Hannah could speak to me about her brother and her sadness and her rage.

Covid came and our classes moved to Zoom. One night, she lingered again as the other students logged off.

She was back at home in Florida, and I was in my basement in Virginia with its window onto the backyard. Her surroundings evoked a kind of material security – golden retriever, swimming pool – but her face and voice were full of pain. I could hear my neighbour's chickens and the yells of his children as they played outside on the trampoline. *I just wanted to tell you it's his birthday*, Hannah said. We both cried a little and spoke for some time, our screens glowing brighter as night came in around us.

My own brother had been dead eight years. I could see in Hannah a feeling I had once intimately known: impossibility.

It is a suffocating question: *How will I live without my brother?*

My only answer is my life.

To write to others, I must write my way back to myself.

You will leave the room where it happened.

Your brother's body, made delicate by illness, vacated of his voice and his being. He lies, dressed by the nurses, in blue pyjamas (though you did not see this, you have great faith in their gentleness). You will pass the small Christmas tree in the foyer of the hospice, leave that quiet place made just for dying and get into your boyfriend's car. The motorway is loud beneath you. Winter: the sharp beauty of frost. You leave the car on the brick drive at his grandparents' house in the suburbs and catch the train and then the Tube back to your flat. It strikes you that the world is crammed full of adverts, poster after poster all the way up the escalators. Your vision keeps refocusing. At your flat, your clothes from before hang in the cupboard, waiting to be occupied. You go into your kitchen of cracked tiles and plain white IKEA plates, the clutter of your burgeoning adulthood. You both do and do not believe what has happened. Along the left side of your body – a presence? – a sensation like being touched by the lightest cloth.

A day and then days pass. You burn yourself on soup and look down at the small red continent on your hand. It is a relief to stop being frightened. All through your brother's illness your heart raced; your fool body could never admit there was nothing to be done.

After two weeks, you will open up your notebook. Your last entry was an impossible wish and now you just write, *It has happened.* Then you write your brother's name. You write his first name and his whole name, pressing the thought of him into the page hundreds of times.

Bereavement fresh on you, you attend an event at your university. You step out of the winter evening into an overly bright room, your red boots meeting the parquet, a cup of warm box wine put into your hand. You pose for a photograph, looking like a smiling picture of confidence.

One of your lecturers will tell you tonight, *Work is the great healer*, and you will take this phrase and live beneath its shelter for years.

Soon after this, on the white laptop you bought because it was small and cheap, you'll begin to write something that feels like a novel. It is not so much a project as a place to go. You do not know it yet, but your book has begun its work of keeping you in the world with its small, insistent whisper of, *Finish me*.

In your classes, you perform an impression of yourself. Limbs awkward, your voice comes out from somewhere other than your throat. You expected grief to sadden you but did not know it would make you so strange. That after-the-dentist feeling of the body prickling its way back from sedation. Spring is coming, buds bursting from the branches. The world pulses with beauty for your brother to miss. You cry in the supermarket and on the bus. You stand by a wire pen in the park near your flat, letting the goats lick your fingers. A woman warns you of their teeth and you cry your way home, ashamed.

Your peers are babies. You prefer the elderly, their pragmatism, the soft, collapsing flesh around their eyes. How smooth young people seem, how stupid. You resent their ignorance of death, which is to say, you are painfully jealous, as if in their thirst for fun, their little heartbreaks, they are flaunting something of yours that was stolen. You also sometimes smile down with a kind of patronising benevolence, taking delight in their dramas, listening and listening and thinking, *How wonderful to have a problem that isn't really a problem at all.*

Beware the arrogance of grief. You are not as wise as you think.

For now, your brother has taken the future away with him. You cannot imagine how much more will happen to you. You cannot imagine your life containing anyone you do not already know.

Often, rage.

At the friend who tells you kombucha cures cancer. At your boyfriend's mum, who barely mentions what has happened. Rage at all the people who fail to get in touch. Rage at objects. In a stationery shop, you shake your head bitterly – perhaps even hiss *fuck off* – at a five-year planner; how could one possibly imagine so much future, assume such control? Rage at the acquaintance who, out of polite-ness, asks how your brother is doing in hospital and then visibly steps back when you reply, *He died.* The two of you are standing at a long window waiting for others. It is such a betrayal, that indelible step. After a beat he replies, *I'm sorry*, but he is already looking away. Rage is loneliness.

You also feel an acute new sensitivity to kindness. A friend comes all the way from Paris to visit you at your parents'

house. She lies down next to you in your brother's bed.
His room untouched. By sleeping there she declares that
she is not afraid of him or of you. You will never forget
that she did this.

At six months, you'll get a summer job, which involves
putting things into a spreadsheet: a task for which you
are phenomenally ill-suited. In the office, no one will
know what has happened in your life, you'll just be some
girl. One day a rainstorm will get everyone up from their
desks and they'll stand watching, made briefly child-like
by the extreme weather. And you alone will be returned
to your brother's funeral, when the sky opened just like
this, smashing water against the ground. It will be painful.
But it will also be something else: intimate, suffused with
presence. Afterwards, you'll watch a police horse pick
its way through the puddles on the pavement below,
unhurried. And your brother will rise up to you, secretly,
in the smell of petrichor.

Secrets: no one knows just from looking that you're
wearing a dead man's coat.

At a wedding, you create a strange and elaborate dance
routine with your living brother in the carpeted hallway
of a hotel. Laughing with your living family, more than
anything else, makes you feel found. Later, you walk with
your father in a dark garden, hiding without saying so,
after one of his friends remarked, unthinking, *All our
children are here.*

*

You feel protective of your parents. They have shed so much of themselves – flesh and ambition. You also feel envious. They got to make many of life's big choices before being disrupted by death. Often, you are thrown against your bed by sadness and can do nothing but weep for hours, your boyfriend – afraid, bored, patting you – eventually sliding off to watch *Breaking Bad* in the other room. It only ends when exhaustion gathers the strength to pull you into sleep. From here you are supposed to build a life.

And yet you are living. In the dark crush of a punk concert, you dance in that rib-bruising way, lost in your own aliveness. Some days turn up little treasures, bright things so much sharper than happiness.

The end of the first year. How slowly, how suddenly it comes. You will rise early on the morning of the anniversary, wanting to be awake at the exact time your brother died, as if in that quiet you might meet him once more, at the thin point of the dawn.

You will pay your rent, and spend much of your time changing trains, pressing your way through Clapham Junction with the rumpled uniforms of various work-places in your bag. You will finish your degree with a kind of zeal that one day will unnerve you in your own students. And you will write in draughty station cafés and at home in the sanctuary of 4 a.m. It *is* healing, all this effort, and exhausting. It is penance for having been randomly assigned to stay alive.

*

Sometimes all your fevered energy will seep through your pores and whole days will elapse in which you'll do nothing at all but listen to audiobooks in bed, wondering how you'll ever get up again.

It is difficult to find the world moving forwards, remaking itself without regard for the space in which your brother stood. The two of you often climbed a narrow staircase together on Charing Cross Road to sit chatting in the café of Foyles, books filling the floors beneath you. When the shop changes its location, reappearing, newly bright and spacious, a few doors down on the same road, it feels like violence against your private history. You also know, a year and a half into grief, that this feeling is ridiculous. That the world is for living in and cannot be expected to take on the sweet permethrin smell of archives, everything kept in cabinets and touched only by hands in white gloves. During a visit to another country, a pen you lifted from your dead brother's desk runs dry of ink. Your solemnity feels like a private joke as you drop it into the bin. There is some power in it – this falling away of the world he touched. It is like the shedding of a skin, beneath which lies an undimmable sense of him. Though when your boyfriend utters the phrase *moving on* you despise him.

You pick up a title in that new incarnation of the old bookshop, thinking it would make a good gift for your brother. For a second you are shocked once more by the fact of his death. You stand still with the book in your hands and then put it down and walk out into the street.

Sometimes a lighter sort of forgetting: with only half of yourself aware he is dead, you think, *This café, this vanilla cheesecake – I must bring my brother here.*

Every now and then, usually late at night, you read PDFs online of leaflets about sibling grief, which incessantly use the word *normal*. Guilt is normal. Normal is your bottomless sadness. Nothing has ever made you lonelier.

You graduate. You wear his mortarboard. You cry at the ceremony with a mad woman's pride.

And then in the third year, something strange begins to happen. It manifests at first in the desire to curl your hair. You stand at a bright glass counter in a make-up shop with your living brother. All around you, plastic and pigment and a smell like wax crayons. On this day you buy a pale-pink lip liquid the shade of no human mouth. Because, why not? You put it on and enjoy being glanced at on the train. This vanity is your life coming back for you.

It is a shock to realise you are still young. You have been young all this time.

*

At some point you will begin to have fun again. Quietly at first. And it will astonish you, your whole body atingle with disbelief. You had thought you'd forever be living behind glass.

When you left the hospice and climbed wordlessly into your boyfriend's car it seemed like a promise to be with that boy for life. How, you had wondered, could you ever leave someone who had sat beside your brother watching history documentaries, had known him before illness? Someone who had brought you a soft and comfortable change of clothes at the hospice and had, for love of you, entered the room of death?

But here's how: realise, joyfully and guiltily, that life is long for most of us. You *are* young and might take a young person's mundane risks. Curl your hair and fall in love with someone else. Have terrible conversations. Cry on the train. It is almost satisfying to know that for once the strangers who think, *Break-up*, at the sight of your young woman's tears will be right.

On a crisp inevitable day, you become older than your big brother ever got to be. But he keeps his place up ahead of you by being dead, retaining his elder authority.

The world is still littered with sparks of his presence.

Work, your companion and healer, begins to bear good things. You hold in your hands a contract with your name on it beside the word *writer*. You take a train to a small town to accept an envelope containing £200 for one of your poems. Your brother believed wonders like this would befall you. And so, you tell him, *I'm doing it*, inside your mind as you walk to the front to claim your prize.

You will fling yourself at new love, and your heart will break. It will be awful and kind of good. You thought grief had made you wise to the world, as if that one great shock had used up all your earthquakes. Yet here you are, pining for some man! Pleasure of a pain that will pass. Blood pooling in your heart, the meat of it torn but beating.

You have become less volatile, less in need of escape routes. It is a reprieve that gives you a false confidence. Child, you are about to lose your mind.

Because grief is not linear. You can make *progress*; you can dance at a festival, churn up the grass, music in you and the evening cool after a hot day; you can feel like an ordinary twenty-six-year-old, except with a greater access to joy, because you know joy's absence, you know about the randomness of life, that both crises and delights are the fruits of chance; you can wear lipstick and work and work. And then, when you least expect it, you can fall into despair.

*

Your great healer fails you. You learn that work, the salve of activity, can only do so much. You mistook the force, which led you this far, for strength, when it was in fact the carrying power of a shockwave. There will be long, bleak months which you fear you won't survive.

You will emerge quieter and more adventurous.

And in this crude state, you will finish the first whole draft of your novel. Years later, you will read the line from Sinéad Gleeson, 'I'm not going to die, I'm going to write a book,' and it will make you cry. She uttered these words on the night of her leukaemia diagnosis. We cannot choose the outcome of illness, but Gleeson tells us we can commit to art and in so doing commit to living.

You move four thousand miles away and populate your life with people your brother never knew.

Your life in London another skin shed. And once more, beneath it, you find that your brother remains, his absent presence still so vibrant. The thing about him is, he is everywhere.

In your new country, you do laundry in the basement of your apartment, counting out unfamiliar coins for the machines. One cold morning, steam infused with the chemical-floral scent of laundry soap spills from the vent by the stairs. You pass through it like an aeroplane through cloud. Holding your warm, clean clothes, you are struck by the miraculous notion that you are likely to grow old.

Your friend Lee writes to you because his own brother has died. And with every single word you write back, you go climbing over the days and years towards yourself in your own first weeks of grief. You tell Lee that *make* is an erroneous verb in the non-question, *Perhaps you know how to make it easier?* Easier just happens. Easier comes, extending and retracting its way through one's life. You tell him that you often used to weep with little provocation, sometimes briefly and sometimes uncontrollably for hours, but you do not do that any more. And now that danger has stopped coming, you realise that you do not regret your weeping because the alternative – attempting to ignore your sadness into submission – would have been worse. Through the years when thinking of your brother made you furiously sad, you still chose to think of him. And he has repaid the loyalty of your keeping him close. So, you tell your friend, keep hold of your brother and he will adjust his position on your body. He will make himself easier to bear.

When did this happen, you wonder, your brother lighter on your back? At some point you seem to have set so much of your fury down.

Someone you used to know died, also young and of cancer. You once chastened this person in your mind for not reaching out to you with condolences, though you knew nothing of their life. You are so ashamed. And you learn that someone you love lived through something horrifying years before you met. You go into the mountains and stand in a stream, thinking of your foolishness as the water flows cold around your shins. How naive it is to assume your own heart the most broken in the room. How unkind. You are in your late twenties, realising that hard things have not only happened to you.

Not long after the email from Lee, another friend gets in touch, this time on WhatsApp. He has similar questions but the being that has died is his dog. You would once have been infuriated. For a long time, you guarded grief, privately dismissing those mourning grandparents and pets. But you have begun to care less about hierarchies of loss. You picture your friend's dog, a streak of brown-gold light, dashing over Streatham Common, his belly brushing the grass, and remember feeling his quivering body against your leg the time you all concealed him in a holdall to travel home from a party in an Uber. If he is gone from the world, that time in all of your lives is more definitively the past.

You tell your friend that the most beautiful word you know is *and*.

People use *but* in relation to death. He is dead, *but* I am going to have a good life. I miss him, *but* I shall always remember him. Etcetera. *But* poses things as opposites, as if the second halves of those sentences could ever negate the first. You much prefer, he is dead, *and* I am going to have a good life. I miss him, *and* I shall remember him. Because we have to carry both realities. We can.

It has been six years. Another summer comes and you swim in a pond with a friend. You're laughing, made a little wild by the occasional touch of unseen plants against your legs. You tread water and talk. She is also a writer, and her draft novel is about love, though, she jokes, it has made her no wiser on the subject. You have just sold your book to a publisher, and this feels both like the fruit of a lot of work and the manifestation of an absurd birthday-candle wish. *Our books don't teach us anything*, you laugh. *I still think I'll be able to take mine down to the underworld and swap it for him.* A silence passes between you across the water. You had not known this, but it's true.

You still write his name in notebooks.

And just once, you see him. Seven years after his death, you will be standing in line at a salad bar in a town in a country your brother never visited. You'll turn your head and glimpse him there. This place was overwhelming when you first moved here. It is always packed, and one must order very quickly to keep the line moving and speak up to be heard through the glass separating customers and servers. It was here that you realised that in the US, *How are you?* is not a question, but a greeting. Today, you will near the front of the line, turn your head and see him, clearly, standing at the door. You'll know it the second you turn your head back. You will feel your heart land, as if dropped very carefully into your chest. Then you'll look again, and he'll be gone.

You don't believe he was really there, which is to say that the words *believe* and *really there* are unhelpful in this context. He came shining through your memory and, for a moment, the present thinned enough for you to see him, more palimpsest than ghost.

You told Lee that people would piss him off, by saying stupid things or saying nothing at all or simply continuing to exist, unaware of how hard life can be. That grief for an untimely death can be very lonely. But the thing is, the loneliness doesn't last. Because most people are coming this way. Those who don't yet understand offer the world necessary lightness. And when they do arrive at loss, we who arrived early will be standing here to meet them.

You make a new friend whose sister just died. A strikingly gentle person. He never asks you the kind of questions Lee asked, and you would never presume to advise him. This is the opening of a space in which you do not have to be wise. Where neither person has to know how to survive, only that you are doing it together. When you are given the chance to give a reading at a bookstore, you tell him not to come in case your writing makes him sad. He says, *I am willing to be sad*. Now here's a house you might live in.

Flowers arrive on the day you marry him, bouquets appearing on your doorstep and brought over in jars by friends. You return from the courthouse via a cheap Mexican restaurant. The taste of sweet horchata on your lips, you stand in your living room surrounded by vases. *All these flowers, like a death*, you think at first. And then, *All these flowers, like a meadow*.

Now here comes Hannah, standing in your classroom one evening after the others have left, waiting to explain her strangeness. You remember how this felt, the need to account for your volatility, to come out as bereaved. The hours you spend speaking with her and exchanging long emails are not at all selfless. She is an undergraduate, just as you were when your grief began. Your conversations are vaguely pedagogical; you cannot help but want her to write because she is good at it. But in her a part of you is making the friend your younger self longed for.

You tell her that the funny thing about time is that it does not only run forwards.

Your brother, dead nine years, never seems to get further away. You still note funny things to tell him, jokes filed away as if the two of you will be meeting later on. It is not that you forget that he is dead. It is that there is a lovely fold of your brain in which this fact will simply never be relevant.

You write in a notebook, *I don't believe in time*, adding this thought to your gathered amulets of language (that passage from *Angels in America*, Marie Howe's clogged sink, 'To a Dead Graduate Student' by Thom Gunn. These things you have reached for in the dark and merged into a single rambling prayer). You think you made it up.

Then one day you discover these lines from Vladimir Nabokov: 'I must confess, I do not believe in time. I like to fold my magic carpet, after use, in such a way as to superimpose one part of the pattern upon another. Let visitors trip.'

Long ago your brother wrote in a notebook of his own, *I am afraid that my family will never be happy again after this. I have to believe that they will be.* And so, you fold your magic carpet and tell him, *I am.*

I am happy, John.

Sometimes, still, an incision is made by memory or by language. Ten years on you chance upon these words by Virginia Woolf, 'I have never found a lullaby capable of singing him to rest.' For a moment the sheer unfairness of his death is as fresh as ever, as bright as blood. And then the next moment comes, as you knew it would.

*

You do not believe in time, *and* you have great faith in it. It was time that carried you here and will carry you on.

So, fold back your magic carpet and meet yourself. Tell of what lies ahead. You will find friends in this territory. Lee is going to ask you, *Perhaps you know how to make it easier?* And later he will tell you he is going to become a father. Years and thousands of words into your loss, Hannah will ask, *Have you ever tried to write about it?* Later still, she'll email to ask what that line was *about time being a magic carpet.*

And she will tell you this: *It is like I walk in step with each version of me. It's like every year, the first version of me who was alone and unknowing gains a person. And so, over time, it feels less like I am walking this path alone.* The way things fold, she is so often the older, wiser one.

Go back and say: I know you have stopped believing in the future, but here it is.

At Home

I woke far from home, Luke's sleeping shape beside me in the dark. I slid my hand over the wall of the tent to the mesh pocket where I had stashed my things, ready for this moment. My phone lit up in my palm. It wasn't yet 4 a.m., but no matter, I knew what I was going to do. Unzipping the door, I stepped out onto the plain. Dust soft under my trainers, the sky dark blue. This little campsite seventy miles from the nearest town. The moon full and stars ridiculous in their brilliance. The vast silence of Chaco Canyon.

Two days before, I had been whacked by exhaustion in Santa Fe, an old mountain city where the dry heat made the skin across my face feel tight. As they often do when I need them, a bookshop appeared, and I dived inside to shelter from the sun. Gripping a shelf to stay upright, I thought, *What's happening to me?*

Now, I thought I knew, though I tried to hold that knowledge casually, ready to be wrong.

Strangers breathed around me, behind the walls of their tents. I walked carefully between the guy ropes, protective of their dreaming. Near here, petroglyphs preserved the work of ancient hands. I had felt in company standing below them earlier – the cluster of horned animals and a figure with a spiral shield. I reached the path and aimed the beam of my headtorch at the ground. We had seen the grey corpse of a night snake there in daylight. It had slipped into the dust like a strand of spaghetti when we tried to move it aside with a stick. At my back, the Fajada Butte loomed in the distance, a great flat-topped hill of rock, which we had nicknamed *God*.

At the breeze-block toilet, I opened the door and flicked on the bare-bulb light. I washed my hands with the sharp green soap of National Parks bathrooms, unwrapped the pregnancy test, uncapped it and peed on the part that looks like a tiny tab of sugar cane. It turned pink and then almost immediately a blue cross formed in the window.

A quake of calm passed through me.

As I walked back to the tent, the day was just beginning to arrive, touching the jagged edges of the plain. Had I ever had an experience so entirely private? A new person was coming towards the world, and I alone knew.

I unlocked the car and sat in it writing notes, as if the thing to do now was record the bleed of light from behind the rocky hills. This was where Luke found me.

I'm pregnant, I told him.

When we tell people the story, we skip a line and go straight to the second thing he said, because it gets a laugh: *That's pretty scary*.

But in fact, he first said, *Really?*

And I said, *Yes*.

*

How did you know, Katie once asked me, *that you wanted
a child?*

I thought about it. It had been a bodily longing,
like hunger or thirst, which had simply grown stronger
over time. It had also come as a command as I walked
through the hospice on the hushed winter morning of
John's death. How blunt the human survival urge is, the
thought, *Have a child*, falling into a space its exact size
in my brain. *But it's something else too*, I told her, *like . . .
being haunted . . . but by the opposite of a ghost?* What I
meant was that for years I had felt the surface of life thin-
ning, as if I might with my ordinary hands pinch the first
layer of things, make a little tear, and allow something
else through.

I continued travelling through the American Southwest
that summer, feeling altered and somehow more impli-
cated in all that I saw: the families of prairie dogs in
the sand by the stoplights; the steep, silty hills of cacti
and mountain sage, which smelled sweetly of piss; the
armoured back of a dead armadillo on the road. I kept
the pregnancy test in my backpack and often drew it out
surreptitiously, sure I had misread its chemical rune. In
a general store in Utah, I bought a second test and the
brass-blonde older woman who rang it up said, *Congratulations either way*, smiling but toneless.

Then there was the fact again in a restaurant bathroom:
pregnant.

Christine, by wondrous coincidence, was also pregnant. She flew out to meet us at the Needles, a park named for its hundreds of skinny spires of rock, and we sat in the car attempting to keep the blowing sand out of the dinner we were preparing, cutting vegetables on boards on our laps. When clearing stones to pitch the tent, I had tugged the green nub of a plant and pulled out the whole long body of a lizard, dead but still bright green, buried vertically in the sand. It seemed a little reckless to be out here in the desert with these new clusters of cells inside us. My hurriedly downloaded pregnancy app told me the embryo was the size of a grain of salt. *Hold on, little salt*, I thought as we all climbed a slope of slickrock to look down on the campsite from above, Luke springing ahead and Christine and I edging sideways, freshly cautious. Floes of dust swirled below us as the sun set, then out came the bats, drawing quick patterns through the twilight. The next day, the heat broke into a flash flood, and we ran for shelter, lightning chasing us, striking the ground before our eyes, an electric, metallic taste in the air.

I had read about these landscapes, had seen pictures of them, yet found myself unprepared for their mind-bending reality: layered worlds of rock all the way to the horizon at Canyonlands and Capitol Reef, impossibly connected like an Escher staircase, my eyes falling upon another level every time I thought I'd found the bottom; Petrified Forest National Park, where the trees had alchemised to stone and the sand around them shone eerie white like the skin of another planet.

My salt grain grew into a raindrop, then a tadpole-like creature with a tail. The image on the app looked like the wriggling lives we saw in a pool in Zion National Park: a place of stunning beauty, overrun with sunburnt families and fat, aggressive squirrels who had developed a taste for sandwiches. My breasts felt different. Pregnancy began announcing itself in a heightened sense of disgust, my mouth musky and sour. I spat out a leathery glob of soy jerky in revulsion and for days its taste was my first thought upon waking. In Arizona we met up with a group of friends and friends of friends and I found that I didn't want to speak to anyone, only to sit in silence in the 40-degree Celsius heat of our campground, moving my eyes over the dust and scrub plants and the distant irregular shapes of the mountains. Then one afternoon, emotion: a flash flood. Alone in the tent, I sobbed for hours. It was distinct from my weeping in grief: chemical. I remembered the force with which puberty had crashed through me, how frightening that had been, the sense of being picked up and thrown by a thing beyond my control.

We had called the trip our honeymoon, two years and a pandemic after our wedding, a one-word spell, which justified travelling so far and for so long, and the extravagance of so much beauty. Leaning over the railing of the Grand Canyon, I struggled to comprehend its vastness until I saw people trekking into its depths, small as seeds in the hollow belly of the earth. That afternoon, I saw a jackrabbit, huge and with something canine about its hindquarters. It emerged into my field of vision as its cousin the hare had once done on the misted path of the River Thames. Alert but unafraid, it was as magnificent as the canyon but stranger, because it watched me back.

How was I going to maintain my awe after this trip, I wondered? Would the future be endless jackrabbits, met with diminishing amazement? But I knew the deer, which were so common at home in Virginia, had never stopped amazing me with their clumsy elegance and watchfulness, the clean white of their tails. And I was yet to outgrow my awe at the fireflies that arrived in our yard each June. A child was coming (a cautious part of me added *probably, perhaps*) for us to show the world to.

We started for home. Two thousand miles and four long days of driving. The 'baby' was the size of a bean. From the car in Tucumcari, New Mexico, I watched a middle-aged man drag an enormous wooden cross along the edge of the road, nausea roiling within me. I checked motel mattresses for bedbugs and stuffed dry bran flakes into my mouth when I woke, trying to outpace the morning sickness, which intensified with hunger but made the thought of eating grim. In stores, everything my eyes fell upon appalled me: apples – disgusting; dry rice in a packet – disgusting. Bread somehow, beneath the billowing air conditioning and bright lights of the supermarket, smelled of sweat. I only wanted colourless warm foods. Mashed potatoes from Cracker Barrel, a roadside chain with wagon wheels on the wall and a gift shop, like a tiny theme park of an imagined old America. White, watery grits from Waffle House, where in Missouri, a waitress greeted a customer as *Sir*, and another cried, *Oh, that ain't no sir, that's just Tadpole*. As the days passed, and the dry heat slowly shifted to humidity, I spent more and more time leaping from the car to puke white foam, buckled on my hands and knees in parking lots.

At last, we pulled up in front of our magnolia tree in Virginia, its stiff, dark leaves perspiring in the heat. I did not feel at home in my body, but it was a relief to retreat inside and surrender to my strangeness.

School and the movies had taught me more about the conditions of war than of pregnancy. I felt naive when that first trimester floored me, utterly unprepared for the days spent horizontal and groaning with nausea before crashing into bed in all my clothes with unbrushed teeth. The nights of waking at 3 a.m., feral-alert, and sniffing through the dark house before falling asleep again at sunrise on the living-room rug. The world stank; could no one else smell that gross pollen ripeness, rot simmering below the surface of verdure? Food grew even more horrific, and in a notebook from this time lies the command, *Drink fluids!* followed by the fearful note: *I can't start finding water disgusting, I simply cannot.* I begged Luke, *Please don't talk to me about tea. Don't talk about green peppers.* Dry heaving over the toilet bowl, I became well acquainted with the scents of piss and bleach. How would I do this, I fretted – the cell by cell building of a child – were it not for my teaching job and its long summer break? And what would happen when the semester began?

But none of this was the real problem. My mind seemed like an object I had put down somewhere, never again to be found. I felt lazy, blank. Like even the small things I had achieved in my life had been done by someone else. I couldn't imagine writing more than a few scrawled notes ever again. Frightened, I pored over articles on pregnancy – 'Ten Weird Early Pregnancy Symptoms No One Tells You About: You'll taste metal! You'll pee all the time!' – but this disconcerting blankness was never mentioned beyond vague references to *brain fog*. It was as if I alone had encountered this or that the ability to think was somehow an irrelevance for women. I thrilled at the changing pictures on my app, the two tiny buds forming, ready to become arms. The being nested beneath the guarding bones of my pelvis had been longed for, and that longing was already a sort of love. But I felt a kind of dread I couldn't articulate. Unable to write, I would attempt to read, and exhaustion would blast through me, whiting everything out like a blizzard. Gum-mouth and gum-brain, I yearned to come home to my mind.

At the first ultrasound all the pictures on the wall in the clinic were of landscapes. The technician called me *Mom*. I imagined her discovering that something had gone wrong and having to tell me that my insides were empty, that word unretractable between us, as if I might outfox this fate by thinking it before it could happen.

But there it was: the grey shape of the foetus and within it the smaller pulsing shape of a beating heart, so quick. My own heart quickening, racing to catch it. *It's moving!* Luke said. *Does it have muscles?* Laughter and relief: in this moment, at least, our baby was real. Shimmering. I was allowed to believe it.

I waited in another room to be examined, thinking of birth, that frontier. I had watched a video online for this clinic's birth centre: long drone shots over bright lawns and the promise of valet parking, attractive couples checking in, hair and teeth shining, not a hint anywhere of pain. I felt my vast ignorance of American hospitals and a pang for the dowdy compassion of the NHS, not customer service but care. An acquaintance had warned me not to accept a coffee after the birth: *they'll charge for that.* Was she joking? I sat on the examination bench in the thin purple gown I'd been given and noticed that this room too was decorated with prints of fields and flowers. *Am I meant to do this as a woman,* I wondered, *or as a meadow of poppies?*

I turned my scant energy to researching places to give birth: an act both logical and tinged with magical thinking, as if my hours squinting at data and scratching little notes might earn me something, cast some protection around my choices. In *The Lancet*, I found a meta-analysis of the outcomes of 500,000 births; it suggested that in my circumstances a home birth could be safe. I held that data close, as in the past I'd held lines of poetry, and went to meet Kelly, a home-birth midwife. Her qualifications hung on the walls of her one-room practice, alongside images of bellies and blooming placentas and a ferocious-looking woman with her legs apart and several tiny fierce babies tumbling from her into the world. Yes, it was all rather *goddess*, rather unironic, but did I really plan to give birth ironically, one eyebrow raised? Kelly was calm and in possession of a certain ready humour that I have encountered only in deeply serious people. With her, I felt safe.

And for all my assessment of percentages, risks, I was also just ready, at last, to believe that death and danger were not uniquely trained upon my family. Determined to believe this, in fact. After John died, twenty-five and as spare as bone, slipping away from us through a morphine haze, and then once more during my mother's illness, I had wondered how I would ever again feel safe, the question itself frightening, safety a vital lost object that I must tear the house up to find quickly or never at all. But I am not superstitious. Unspeakable loss was no more likely for me than for anyone, it was simply more imaginable. And I was a writer. I could imagine other things. So, I imagined having my baby in my little house at the dip between steep hills, here in Virginia, where I had planted irises and ruffle-edged tulips and daffodils. It would mean no epidural and (because it's rarely used in the US) no gas and air. But my curiosity rushed out ahead of my fear.

The grimness in my body lifted. An incremental wonder. I stopped vomiting, then stopped sniffing food suspiciously before I ate. I taught, wondering when I should tell my students; my body was still inconspicuous but for my one red cheek and the creases in my clothes from sleeping heavily on the carpet in my office before class. And then one day, standing in the street, my mind made a few simple connections – that book, this memory, the yellow gingko leaves on the pavement – and I realised with a rush of joy that I was *thinking* again.

Soon after this, Kelly drew my blood and sent it away to be examined for chromosome traces of the baby's sex. The ritual a few weeks on was familiar from our many postal Covid tests: sitting on the sofa with Luke, we logged on to a portal and clicked *show result*. Afterwards we tried to carry the word *female* lightly, to remember that more than anything our child would be themself. But it was something to imagine, a reason to feel a firework flash of happiness when 'My Girl' by the Temptations came on in a coffee shop. *Where do I know this feeling from?* I wondered. It was falling in love: the tumbling sensation, emotional and bodily, corny old songs given a lick of fresh meaning.

Then one afternoon, the magic of movement. Subtle but unfamiliar enough to be unmistakable. Something tiny and aquatic rolling over inside me.

It was 2021. Autumn. In my classroom we still all wore masks. I read fairy tales with my students – Rapunzel's pregnant mother craving lettuce then Rapunzel herself pregnant in her tower, tales of children given away by parents wilfully or through stupidity, of longed-for babes born strange, covered in prickles – fear and yearning rippling through each word. A tornado warning sent Luke and me into the basement. We lay on our camping mattress and watched through the glass door as the weather beat the world, hoping our tall black walnut tree wouldn't crash through our roof. It was exciting and we were afraid. And what were we doing, having a child? Wasn't despair most appropriate, in this world, in the face of the pandemic and the irreparable wounding of the Earth? Could we have reasoned ourselves out of it somehow, our wish to make a life? The tenacious hope that just maybe we had not arrived in history too late. Luke touched my swollen stomach, over it a new soft layer of fine hairs. Upstairs on our fridge was a list of names.

Across the country in Chicago, Christine's stomach bloomed outwards at the same rate as my own, our babies due within days of one another. Both were apparently the size of *a small avocado*, then *a squash*, then *a large marrow* and, according to the NHS website, *the weight of six large carrots*. Phone calls came from across the world. The WhatsApp line glitched along the miles between Virginia and Marseille as my friend Holly told me she was also pregnant. As children we had stained our tongues blue in the park by the sweetshop. I had got into trouble at her house for squashing the soap by squeezing it too hard in my little fist and when I slept over in her bedroom, her mum had bent and kissed us both in the dark. She was due in May, and I was overjoyed for her. I also felt a mote of sadness; if we were both to be mothers, that girlhood truly was over. Sometimes we want our friends to stand still in the place we have moved away from, keeping it in reserve: a fantasy of a return to the past. My best friend Rachel still lived in a house we had once shared in London. Her voice full of laughter, she called to say she was pregnant too.

My body was conspicuous and full of secrets. A stranger glanced at me and said, *Congratulations*, when we crossed in the street. The first signs of milk appeared, not dripping but in crystals, tiny yellow-white peaks, like an expression of salt on rock. My daughter's movements became visible on the outside, my belly rippling like the surface of a lake. I read and obsessively listened to podcasts, needing voices, to hear other women say, *Here's how I tore and here's how I applied witch hazel, this is how much it hurt, and this is the kind of bassinet I bought.* Pregnancy is all change and all suspension, a desert stretching between one's known life and something unimaginably different. And so, I washed and folded tiny second-hand clothes sent to us from Luke's enormous family, knitted a grey blanket destined to remain ever unfinished, and removed the corpse of a vole from our basement, readying our small house in this huge, borrowed country I had only ever planned to pass through.

*

The new year came and we woke to a world transformed. A snowstorm came with fierce beauty and took our power out for days. The pregnancy had begun in the desert, the horizon warped with heat, and I was entering its final movement, my third trimester, wearing my coat, gloves and hat to bed and clinging to Luke for warmth. White blasted through our windows, and I thought about how close to the edge of things we were and had always been. Our house suddenly seemed fragile, stripped of heat, no life in the lights and sockets. The pandemic had changed us. Now, when small and fixable catastrophes came, we wondered, *Is this what it would be like?* if an apocalypse came for real.

But motherhood had been growing within me alongside my child. Christine was visiting. We could hardly hug with our two bumps between us. *Well, this is what it would be like*, I thought, as she and I made a meal with shivering hands on the flame of a camp stove, the back door open to the cold to stop the gas fumes gathering in the house. This is what it would be like, at least in part: giving the care we could muster, being homes to our children, helping and being helped.

At the very end of the pregnancy some of the early exhaustion returned, the baby at work in my body, filing my bones to spindles. I had no maternity leave – I was in America after all – and taught a class on my due date. When I paused at the blackboard, touched my belly and grimaced, a student's eyes bulged, worry written all over his face that I might be about to get down on the ground and give birth there and then.

But days later, when it actually started, it was unmistakable. I woke to a squeezing sensation. Firm rather than painful. It was 2 a.m. and all was quiet beyond the bedroom curtains, no cars coming down the hill. I looked at the two pink tablets on the nightstand, which Kelly had given me to aid sleep if it began like this; on no account was I to succumb to excitement and get up. I swallowed the tablets and lay in the dark on my side, half sleeping through the beginning of the end of the pregnancy, a hand to my big belly, feeling the lump of my daughter's now-familiar foot, trying to slow my mind and my breath. I did not wake Luke. There was nothing for him to do yet in these quiet hours and I needed him strong for what lay ahead. It was as it had been in Chaco Canyon at the beginning. Our child was coming, and for this short while, I alone knew.

Because labour is not typically as it is in the movies – a flood of fluids, then screaming, all over in the space of a montage – we went out for breakfast. Beside a cabinet of sugared doughnuts, the pinch of another contraction came, small but clear as the striking of a bell, my wince a secret shared between us. I lived that March day as softly as I could, dancing through my neighbourhood with one foot in the road and the other up on the kerb because I had read it could open the pelvis, attempting to sleep, simmering tomatoes and beans in the kitchen, music and the scent of cumin rising around me and steam on the faces of the cupboards.

And all the while I felt that the future had snaked back to get me – us – each contraction another tug along its irreversible path.

Then it really began. I had read about birth and seen pictures of it but when the sun went down, I entered an unimaginable landscape.

My belly was lumpen, pulsing, tight, the baby all squashed at the bottom of the bump. Pain. Luke held the phone up for Kelly to listen as I went through a contraction, the low moan like no sound I had ever made, no sound I could voluntarily recreate. She got in her car, rain falling through the dark. Kelly and her assistant, Sara, arrived and laid out supplies across our piano stool: pads for the absorption of blood and fluids; clean, mysterious implements on a metal tray; two white mixing bowls from our kitchen lined with plastic bags, one for the placenta, one for possible vomit. They began to inflate the birth pool, the two of them methodical, all pragmatism, so that I might be all instinct.

I had to keep moving, circling the living room, slipping outside onto the porch to watch the rain, which overspilled the gutters, heavy as the day we buried John. I was boiling in my black nightgown, my hands swollen, my feet thickly veined on the concrete – so much blood in them, in all of me – my hair scraped back, my breasts huge and heavy, sweating with my eyes half closed. Back inside the house and into the bedroom, burrowing into the mattress with my face squashed and my bottom up – a position with the echo of sex, Luke pressing his big hands against my hips – then lying on one side on the cheap, staticky sheets we had bought to protect the bed, below them a layer of plastic – discovering that lying down was most painful of all and clambering up to stand with one foot astride the bed, then hobbling out to loop the living room once more – climbing onto the sofa we'd covered in old towels before retreating into the little cave of the bathroom to crouch over the toilet where Sara pushed down firmly onto my knees.

It was soon apparent that all my preparations, my months of squatting on my heels every time I brushed my teeth, nights of clutching ice cubes after dinner, working up to holding them for a whole minute, were puny in the face of this pain. *Move, move*, my body said. The assertion was familiar from the determined shuffling walks I had forced on myself during my spell of madness, but now it was undeniable, though movement was difficult. Each position was an utterance, a question in my long discussion with the pain. Each position was a step, an attempt to travel forward through its maze. I pictured my three pregnant friends, lined up behind me on the path to this place. *Oh no*, I thought, on all fours, pressing my shins and forearms and forehead against the cool bathroom floor, my ponytail flopping forward onto the tiles, *I have to tell the others not to do this.*

And yet, between agonies, the immense pleasure of relief. I had been feasting on information for months and had repeatedly googled, *What do contractions feel like?* knowing all the while I was asking too much of my old ally, language. And, yes, the words I had read for the pain – *cramping, squeezing, pressure* – were inadequate against its reality, belonging too much to the world of common things. But those hundreds of words had also failed to capture the moments without pain. I had read, *Try to rest between contractions.* I had never imagined that over and over again I would get to enter the tiny heaven of my life's worst pain being over. That sweetness. Humming to myself with my eyes closed as Luke played sparse notes on the piano. Agony, then laughter. A cloth to my brow, coolness. Grunting, then pausing to dance, fists loosening into flat palms, which I held to my stomach. Leaning on the doorframe, like I might push the house down. Clutching a bowl, ready to vomit. Resting my head on Luke's chest. That which my mind had reckoned with for years had come with force this night to claim my body: the shock of how hard life can be. And the shock of how lovely.

When Kelly finally said, *You can get in your pool now,* I climbed in clumsily using Luke's shoulder for support. It was the most pleasurable experience of my life, letting that warmth accept me, there in our living room by the piano and the houseplants in gentle shadow, lit by lamps. I let my arms drift in the water, then swished them very slowly. Joy of having skin, of this contained space being just for me. And when the next contraction came a little of the pain that had stormed against my edges seemed to flow out into the water. I felt enlarged, more able to take it.

Many months before, in Kelly's office backing onto a slope of tall trees, I had recounted my family history and she had seemed taken aback, as medical people always are, at the incongruity nestled among the expected facts: a brother dead, so young, to a disease so unlikely. *No*, I had told her, *no genetic cause, no reason ever found*. I had wondered then whether John might somehow help me when this night came, the part of him that lived in my brain and my bones, because I would be glancing up against the beyond into which he had vanished. Luke's sister too, all our dead. Writing this, I remember John engaged in the effort of dying, his brow drawn in concentration, and I think also of my granddad saying in the final hour of his life, *I want to die, but I don't know how to do it*, and my uncle's response, funny and beautiful to me: *I don't think I can help you with that, but would you like a cup of tea?* All that effort, which is, in fact, surrender.

The dead did help me as I laboured. A singular thought came shining, clear as a coin, through the pain: *I get to do this because I am alive.*

I stood on trembling legs in the water for Kelly to press the Doppler to my bump. Sound of our girl, the whoosh of her blood echoing through me, a reminder that she was real, on her way to us. And me so much less eloquent than that quick, steady rhythm; in a snippet of video taken by Sara, I cry out, *She is coming!* and then inexplicably, *She is so cool.*

The night was passing. It must have been, though to me it might have been any time. I had written, 'All the world began with a yes' (a phrase from Clarice Lispector), on a piece of white card, having learnt once long ago, when I lost my mind and screamed *no* into an indifferent city street, that *no* does nothing when the only path is through. Now I lurked in the water, the contractions quieter for a while, and tried to speak back a *yes* to every *no* that revolted against the pain. *Yes*, bring me this child. *Yes*, carry her to me along this hurt. In a moment of clarity, I had told Luke to make the midwives tea, calling him back to the edge of the pool to add, *Give them the Hobnobs*, and they sat in the kitchen, giving me space, their quiet talk at the edge of my consciousness, their occasional laughter. Luke lay on the sofa, exhausted.

The pressure all through my body mounted until my belly and my bottom seemed ready to split. I felt close to puking, to expelling the world's most explosive torrent of shit, but I did not feel close to meeting my child. My waters had still not broken and when I remembered this fact, the baby sealed away from me behind that membranous wall, I despaired. I could not match it, the scale of what needed to happen. My bones would need to bend and all my flesh to break. My cry of, *I can't do it*, brought

Kelly in from the kitchen. Then I slipped again into the world beyond language and was all sound, sound using me, coming not from but through me from some hot place in the centre of the Earth. After a violent contraction, I leant over the edge of the pool and sobbed, *I want my mum.* Language came to rescue me, a fierce, funny phrase out of my mouth before I had time to think it: *I am the mum.*

Laughter. The sweetness of being tended, my face touched and washed. The calm of Kelly and Sara who had been here with so many women before. Luke's fingers in my hair.

Then pain again, lifting me away from my companions; I looked down at them from the thin altitude of what I was scaling, little figures in a trench of canyon.

On all fours I smushed my face into the side of the pool, breasts pendulous and the dark seam down the centre of my stomach straining. I let out a loud, low cry and at the end of it, I felt a pop. *I felt a pop!* I said excitedly. *I felt a pop!*

Relief and joy: my waters had broken at last and this thing in fact was possible. It would end.

This is what it was like when my cervix fully opened: a different tension through me, the set of my shoulders changing, the need to rise up on my haunches, dog-like, thighs braced and forearms pressing the side of the pool, every part of me tautening around the opening, a round feeling with a metal rim, a full silver moon in the slowly opening vice of my pelvis, my face screwed up, muscles locked but mutable, all of me so hard and so soft. Torch-light on the water. Kelly looked under me with a mirror and said she could see the baby's head.

Really?

Yes.

And *yes*, there it was – the hard bone met my fingers. That undeniable head – *Look at all that dark hair*, some-one said – and my body, also undeniable. I was the layer between my daughter and the world. It was impossible and possible and close. I gripped Luke's neck as he held my biceps and I screamed into his face. I *pushed* and was pulled down to the red canyon bottom, the closest one might get to the underworld and come back alive.

Screaming heat and blizzard. The pain and I were one being, with the wild authority of an animal.

No more running: I let the lightning catch me, crackle through my throat and leave my mouth as fire.

I could open no further, her head was coming out.

But then she slipped back.

Inching out again, she held me open, her forehead in the world but her tiny hand up and in the way.

Lucidity: I met Luke's eye, my fingers laced tight around his fist. My body knew what to do.

Push is a soft word after that first plosive thrust, over in the space of a syllable, but what happened next was *expul-sion*, a force that came through me, beyond command. *Expulsion*: a contoured word, a dark-haired thing with bones. She was coming, my ferocious daughter, a bird with an egg tooth. And I had to break to get her out and I didn't care. There was strength in me to rip the ground and drop down below being. I tore open, tore my body and the surface of the world. I tore and I'd do it again to feel such power.

She was out.

She was being passed to me, between my legs.

She was in my arms.

I looked down, my palm around her precious skull, her tiny arms up, a fist still pressed to her mouth. Shock of her, my swollen and slippery girl, her long eyelids, her dark hair wet. Holding her against the outside of myself.

I was helped to rise and clamber out, dripping onto the sofa, which was covered in absorbent pads. The midwives took her just briefly and I worried for a moment about her greyness, her skin a suit too big for her. Then I watched colour come into her, and a little rage. She was brought back to me, and her first latch was sharp as a bee sting. I could feel the determination pulse through her small body. My hand found that familiar foot – it was a jolt to realise it was now on the outside. Already she and I had done something together stronger and stranger than death.

*

Afterwards.

Our first hours in the new world, the long moment of her being. Luke holding her wrapped in a Winnie-the-Pooh blanket against his chest, her tiny back dark with fine hairs. Reflexively, she held onto his finger. I birthed the placenta, which I must write here because it so rarely makes it into the story. Kelly said, *This will be like a big portobello mushroom*, and it came out easily, boneless and dark red, a wonderful emptiness filling my body in its wake. She shone a headtorch between my legs and stitched me up. Then I ate Marmite on toast.

At about five in the morning, after the midwives left and we slid at last into bed, our baby in a bassinet at our side, Luke remembered a small chore he'd forgotten to do and burst into tears, the weight of standing with me through all that pain finally releasing.

Long ago, in another life, it had been like this with another man: my boyfriend at the time of John's death, who collected me from the hospice and drove us home in the snow with quiet calm and tenderness. He too had waited until the lights were out to sob.

What is it like? friends asked.

Oh, I said, knowing I should not try then to bring birth into language, *like a trip to another planet.*

How finely made my daughter was, light shining through her ears on the first day of her life, picking out the red lace of capillaries. Those soft ears, which folded flat against the crook of my arm like pieces of cloth. She dredged me for the orange colostrum, which was more like pollen than milk. I spoke her fresh name. I had never quite believed we would get to keep her. I lived her first days in a delirium, higher than any paper bomb of ecstasy could make me, my nipples like tacks tethering my soft self from floating away.

Then on the fourth night I dreamt of a vivid climate apocalypse and woke up to the clanking together of my breasts. *Clank*: a verb I would never have thought to use for breasts until, with heat and heaviness, my milk came in. After this I felt ragged and courageous and full of appetite. My daughter bashed her head against my chest, and the gesture was a word that meant *more*. One night she crawled up my body in the dark and latched with vampiric strength to my neck. Days vanished into the bud of her small mouth, her breath sweet, conjuring the soft noses of horses. How shockingly human she was. How animal. And me too. I wanted to lick her. Birth had schooled me in my own ferocity.

In the kitchen, our postpartum doula, Cynthia, showed us how to give the baby a bath. The blue plastic tub was perched on our sink beside the draining board. *How does this feel?* Cynthia asked her as she poured water from a cup across the baby's shoulders. *How about this?* I thought of watching John being given a sponge bath in his final days. It had been an unexpectedly peaceful period, though I kept saying, *I just wish we got to keep him.* The light in that room had been gentle too, through the long blinds, and the nurses handled him so carefully, doing only enough. My girl turned her head towards the light, her little bottom against the bench of her bathtub, beside her, our drying dishes.

Around this time, I read a line of poetry by Claire Schwartz: 'One can be with a word, as with a body: Wash it. Accompany it. Be changed by its nearness.' One can be this way with a baby too: pulled by their presence into a different sort of gravity.

Keeping her.

And letting every second fall away.

Her puffs and snores and screaming; her weight, which would only grow; the way she raised her arms on the changing table as if to keep herself from falling; the sweet, stale smell of her urine, like mountain sage; those magic seconds in which our loved kin came journeying through her face: miracles of aliveness. Endless jackrabbits.

I started writing this book before I got pregnant. Then, I had begun to think I'd worked out a few things about life. How to be. But so often now, I feel brand new again.

My daughter came into the world translucent, the under-structures of her face visible. Her fine silk eyebrows seemed embroidered on. But she was also mighty. And she remade me into a creature both stronger than before and more sheer.

Motherhood filled me with questions. When we still counted her life in days, I wondered how I would live now that my being was no longer all contained by the boundary of my skin. And how would I bear such tenderness, a word meaning both care and sensitivity to pain? She was a wound to my attention. My mind roved back to her, just as my hands reflexively sought her soft skull and the velvet of her tiny back. And she devoured time. When would I write? How would I think?

Without maternity leave, I returned to work still bleeding, my organs liable to tumble out into my knickers if I moved too fast. Luke would sit with the baby in my office while I taught. Sometimes, I'd open the door afterwards with a quiet click to find them, a single shadow with the lights off, peaceful in the stillness of early evening. And sometimes I'd reach the mouth of the fourth-floor corridor, hear her screaming and break into a run. Those nights, we'd ask, *How are we going to keep doing this?* Exhaustion grew in me until my whole body tingled with it, like the iced nerve beneath a tooth.

There were times when new motherhood made me feel like a ghost. When waking throughout the night, feeling for which of my breasts was fullest, pulling down my pyjama top and bringing my nipple to my daughter's hungry mouth stripped out my insides and the next day I'd float along behind the buggy like a vacant dress.

I was not shocked by the sheer work of mothering, but how invisible that work seemed to be.

I longed to explain my state but lacked language. For how could I ever speak of that first year of nights? The way the dark lay over me like a pelt to be repeatedly hauled off. The way I gave up on sleep sometimes, the nightlight doubling in my vision, a glowing egg beneath each eyelid as I lay awake. The way I seethed as Luke snored beside me, my jealousy towards him a tear in my heart. The dulling of my days. The months that passed without dreams.

And how could I describe the surety with which my daughter sought me, her perfect body fitting to my own, the keratin bumps on her cheek a constellation, my pride at the way I managed, somehow, to keep meeting her trust. My child excavated more love than I knew was in me and with it a bodily knowledge of my own mother's care; in the hours and years before the dawn of my memory, I too was this completely loved. This intensity of experience seemed somehow unmentionable, perhaps because both the good and the awful were made of mundane parts, their effect cumulative, so few individual moments worthy of recounting.

More than a year has passed since that early dreamtime in which a friend ran her finger over my daughter's newborn palm and said, *You've come such a long way.* She was so strange to us then, a traveller from that most distant place of not being.

Time has revealed that my repetitions of care may feel like an endless loop but are in fact a spiral. I fed again and ran the bath again, ushered her through another wakeful night and added one more packet of baby wipes to the shopping list, and we span forward. She outgrew her very first clothes. One morning, she lay on the bed between me and Luke, looking back and forth at our faces, seemingly amazed, as if just then discovering the fact of our twoness. The blue zippered suit patterned with hedgehogs, which had once seemed ridiculously big, briefly fitted her and made strangers say, *What a handsome little guy*, then I was bundling it away for the thrift store. Her mouth released shining things that seemed to have been waiting, hidden but whole within her: smiles, laughter, teeth. Gesture opened a channel between us. She began to wave hello by extravagantly twisting both wrists.

And then came language, blasting through her like a fever. Ma and Da and a particular hiss we came to recognise as a demand for cheese. She had such appetite to know the world, pointing around the room and demanding, *That's? That's?*

Yes, these are generic miracles. But all love stories are mundane, made up of wonders happening elsewhere and to others, which nonetheless hasten the beating of our hearts.

*

One morning, I walked around my neighbourhood with the baby bound in a grey wrap to my chest. The ends of the lanes were invisible with mist. I knew I would beat this path many times that day, because motion most reliably put her to sleep. Sometimes our walks delighted me, and I'd stand in the mud by a neighbour's fence eating mulberries, feeling nourished, my fingers darkening and my child against my heart. But this morning I despaired. Worn down by care, I was once again walking nowhere. Then I remembered the line by E.L. Doctorow, quoted almost into cliché: 'Writing a novel is like driving a car at night. You can see only as far as your headlights, but you can make the whole trip that way.' Mothering was like this. I trudged forward, not knowing what lay beyond the border of my strength. But if I could just move through this hour and this morning, I would be all right; we would be going the right way.

I touched her little toes one by one. All the way home.

And

Take a left from my front door. Walk four blocks, past the spreading mulberry tree and the corner garden with its spring tide of pink phlox. Turn left again. You'll reach Moore's Creek, a rocky stream with a bridge over it. On the other side lie two paths. One will carry you into a small woodland. The other will lead you along the stream to an old red-brick woollen mill.

We came here almost daily during the long narrow months of the pandemic – what luck to have it – calling back to the bird whose cry sounded like, *Weir-do, weir-do*, hungry for exchange. I know this place in every season. The stream suspended by frost. The cheerful toxic colonies of umbrella-shaped plants, which fill the understory in spring. Summer overgrowth constricting the paths, the air held still by nets of vines, ticks latching to my ankles and, just once, the soft flesh of my upper arm. Breaking out of that relentless heat into autumn's mushroom scent and triumphant colour, movement returning to the air. I walked between these trees heavy with my dreaming child, holding her first in the dark of my body and then in a grey cotton wrap, her face stuck to my chest with sweat.

It is not a place of untouched beauty, this small piece of the world. Rusted pipes cut over the water and trash gathers against the rocks. The pines and walnuts are choked by kudzu and black lotus, plants not native but making a life here. Like me. They proliferate in summer, then die back to a twiggy grey chaff, which hangs forlornly from the boughs for months, a vision of aftermath. Often, I come across attempts at shelter between the trees, abandoned by the time I notice them, a torn blue sleeping bag or the stray parts of a tent. And even when woodland fills my vision, the highway is ever audible beyond the trees, the speeding past of other people's lives as ceaseless as the hushing of the ocean.

But *untouched* is an illusion, isn't it? All the world is entwined with human life and destructiveness. And the last time I boarded the bridge with Luke and our child, a deer stood perfectly still in the silver water. Her edges picked out by light, she looked straight at us, stilling us too.

Take the streamside path and it will carry you under a concrete bridge and over stepping stones, wobbly and slick and impassable after heavy rain. What begins as a straight line between the water and a bank of wild grasses starts to undulate, leading you into a grove of trees. This is where the air starts to reek, sour and acerbic, a smell that goes straight for the throat. Look down – whatever the season, the ground seems speckled with snow. And look up. This is where you'll find the vultures.

The vulture zone smells of death, not the soft mothball sweetness of a dying person's room, but the vigorous odour of decomposition, of process, of these creatures who start with the soft parts, then use their long necks to thrust their whole featherless heads into carcasses, that methodical work expelled as snowy guano on the ground. I know to expect them but still startle at the sight of the vultures. Sometimes one will stretch out a wing, then fold it back in, and there is the occasional burst of orderly commotion as they depart en masse for another tree. But mostly, the vultures are still. A committee of hunched shadows in the branches.

When I see them on the ground, instinct pulls me back. But vultures do not attack people, and in fact have a very high 'imprint risk', making them likely to attach to humans as surrogate parents. They do not spread disease but help to eradicate it from the environment, eating up that which would otherwise fester. They are the earth cleaners. And they are so elegant in flight, rising higher and higher into the sky on currents of warm air, their white-tipped wings stretching up to four and a half feet and beating just once in a while. Their circling silhouettes, ubiquitous in the skies above Virginia, bewitch me, in part because they are not native to my life. And my fascination keeps me young in my adopted country.

What are we to do with the past? I want to make use of that which I am no longer living. To pick at the bones of my life.

*

After I lost my mind and regained it, I developed a fantasy called *the year where nothing happens*: twelve whole months in which no one died, no one close to me became frighteningly ill or hurt, where no one slid off their bicycle onto an oiled road, their rib snapping and spearing the soft meat of their lung. A year without heartbreak, where my mind sat safe in my skull. Without those moments of impossibility when one must step over a tear between the present and whatever is next.

I came closest to my fantasy in the year when I moved countries, which I did blithely, never thinking it would lead to this existence, which, though it only occasionally feels impossible, necessitates living with the ache of a stretched heart.

The year where nothing happens is a relic of another time, made in that old country we all lived in before the pandemic. Before everything we knew was revealed to be so fragile. Before the wars, which have intensified beyond all imagining since I began writing this book – conflicts tethered in my mind to my daughter's short life. For she was a day old and still white with vernix when a bomb hit Maternity Hospital No. 3 in Mariupol. And now, on the phones she tries to take from our hands, we see images daily of children in the rubble of Gaza.

And before my eyes met the charred evidence of climate catastrophe. Before the foggy morning when a friend drove Luke and I down winding mountain roads in California on a 'burn tour'. She pointed out the blackened bellies of redwoods and the empty sites that once held her neighbours' homes, as I sat in the back with the child we'd brought into this world.

It is a self-centred fantasy: *the year where nothing happens.*

It is also a meagre hope for a life. I dreamt it up before *and*, that lovely portable word, which grief taught me to carry closely. Before my present happiness. I once didn't know I could have this: Luke and our daughter, such stinging tenderness.

A final obvious epiphany then: things will continue to happen.

Our daughter was eight months old when a shooting took place at the university where Luke and I both work. I was at the changing table, snapping up poppers over the baby's round little belly, when he came in to tell me. The suspect was still at large, our students hiding in their dorms. And my breath did not catch, and my heart did not race. But dread slipped into the room and began to siphon out the air. *It's the nightmare,* I said, though it came out steadily because I had wondered – how in this country could one not? – whether this day would come.

My classes were quiet in the aftermath. My students seemed so young to me, other people's children with their coloured water bottles on their desks. And yet I felt no wiser than them, as if chance only had elected me to stand at the front. One laid her head down on the desk in a moment of swift despair before picking it up and carrying on with class. One said, *Growing up in America you kind of expect this*, in a voice slackly soft, as if the tendon had snapped inside the sentence.

Living in America means living with the possibility of shocking violence. Guns, present if usually invisible, create an awareness of human volatility, the static of other people's anger. Ordinary things become acts of trust: leaving the house to buy groceries, sitting in the cinema, moving through a crowd. But I do trust. The likelihood of my being directly impacted is still low, though in this country one in five adults have been threatened with a gun, one in five have had a family member killed by a gun and one in five have witnessed another person being shot. The word *trust* has travelled to us from old Norse, via proto-German, and along its path has meant shelter. Trust is not about probabilities but making a place in which to live. I trust my students deeply, though it was a student who pulled a gun from his backpack.

When I picture my daughter starting school in a few years' time, when she will be old enough to carry a small backpack, I try not to think about the very worst acts of violence. Is this the American expression of what all parents must carry, the myriad ways we cannot guarantee our children's safety? In this country, where beauty and rage exist on a scale I feel unmade for, I live at the sharp point of my love.

And on a Tuesday, just before the baby turned one, I received a message at work, which began, *You don't know me, but . . .*, from the housemate of my brother Max, far away in London.

A queasy lightness came over me. I sensed what had happened: not the very worst thing but something dangerously near it. Standing in my office, I called the housemate, who was on a date at a bowling alley at the time. I couldn't hear the sounds around her but filled them in in my mind, the clatter and the grinding roll of heavy balls travelling towards pins and smashing them down. We spoke in steady voices. Max was secure for the moment, in company. I said, *OK, thank you for letting me know.*

Afterwards, I tried to call Max but got no answer, so I walked down the stairs and into the adjacent building and began to teach a class, using my face and voice and the front part of my brain, the rest of me straining towards London, that living piece of my heart, until my call was returned, and I slipped into the hall to take it. Max: their known voice, tinged with the strange hollowness of a person sad but safe, just through the white heat of crisis. Back in my classroom, my students were animated, discussing *The Bachelor.*

That night as I walked past the hospital's emergency room and cancer centre and down the single long road lined with cherry trees that takes me almost the whole way home, I spoke to Max for an hour over WhatsApp. I passed the basketball court, bodies in motion touched by the day's last light.

A thing to be lived with: our inability to part the ribs of those we love, take out their hearts with the utmost gentleness and rinse them of pain. We can only make phone calls, listening from the wrong continent, hoping for the best. And this time, the best is what happened. Max became well again, and as I write they are planting a roundabout in Hackney with unpermitted flowers.

That night, my phone growing warm with our lengthening conversation, I dared to cast a prayer all the way to London.

Max, I said, *we're going to be old.*

And Max said, *Yes, we're going to be old.*

We can't know that, of course, but what a thing it would be.

The vultures came to see us once, on our daughter's due date. I moved with impatient slowness then, heavy, uncomfortable and beginning to imagine the baby as a stubborn thing, clinging to her place within me by her tiny nails. Luke and I came home to find the committee roosting at the side of our house in the walnut trees that stand spindly and ill-formed because they block one another's light. It was March, the trees still leafless, the exposed fractals of their branches stark against the sky. The vultures were still and quiet. We had never seen them here before and there was no sign of anything dead around to summon them. The air was scentless, cold in my nostrils. With the superstition of late pregnancy, I put my hand to my stomach, feeling for the baby, that loved being, out of sight, beneath my skin and slightly parted ribs and stomach muscles, suspended in fluid and never, until we held her, quite real.

Was this a bad omen, we wondered?

But we get to write the stories of our lives. To take what chance offers and shape its meanings into things we can use. And so, we decided the vultures had come to herald change.

The past was ending, clear it away.

Let new things begin.

Works Quoted

'a family from Marshalltown who head-onned and killed forever a man driving West out of Bethany Missouri': Denis Johnson, 'Car Crash While Hitchhiking', *Jesus' Son* (New York: *Farrar, Straus & Giroux*, 1992)

'Tomorrow at dawn, the moment when the land whitens, I will set out. You see, I know that you are waiting for me': Victor Hugo, 'Demain dès l'aube', *Les Contemplations* (France: 1856)

'It was a thing that got away from me – a party I threw in a parentless house': Aimee Seu, 'On Recovery', *Velvet Hounds* (Akron: University of Akron Press, 2022)

'What I did not know when I was very young was that nothing can take the past away: the past grows gradually around one, like a placenta for dying': John Berger, *And Our Faces, My Heart, Brief As Photos* (New York: Pantheon Books, 1984)

'I'm not going to die, I'm going to write a book': Sinéad Gleeson, '60,000 Miles of Blood', *Constellations* (London: Picador, 2019)

'I must confess, I do not believe in time. I like to fold my magic carpet, after use, in such a way as to superimpose one part of the pattern upon another. Let visitors trip': Vladimir Nabokov, *Speak Memory* (London: Victor Gollancz, 1951)

'I have never found a lullaby capable of singing him to rest': Virginia Woolf, *The Waves* (London: Hogarth Press, 1931)

'One can be with a word, as with a body: Wash it. Accompany it. Be changed by its nearness': Claire Schwartz, 'Lecture on Loneliness' (London: Granta Magazine, 2022)

'Writing a novel is like driving a car at night. You can see only as far as your headlights, but you can make the whole trip that way': E.L Doctorow, 'The Art of Fiction No. 94' interview (New York: *The Paris Review*, 1984)

Acknowledgements

I am immensely grateful to my editor Lettice Franklin and agent Jenny Hewson. The two of you embolden me. Lettice, thank you for your precision and insight, and for your perseverance with the pieces which took many drafts to find their way. Jenny, I wouldn't be here without your faith in me. Thank you for assuring me this project was indeed a book, and for guiding me through a publishing deal in the bleary days right after I gave birth.

Thanks and admiration to Mo Johnson and Jensyn Worrell, who took care of my child while I wrote. Without your exceptional work this book would not exist.

Many people are involved in bringing a book to life. Thank you Clarissa Sutherland, Holly Kyte, Javerya Iqbal, Ellen Turner and all at W&N. Thanks to James Nunn and Dan Jackson for the beautiful cover.

An essay tells just one strand of events as they happened, and from one perspective only. My profound gratitude to every person I have depicted in this book, both named and unnamed. You are here because you are important. Thank you especially to Hannah, Learco, Kirsty, Christine, Danny, Rachel, Holly, Luke and Max.

ACKNOWEDGEMENTS

My dear friend Katie Rice both appears in this book and supported the creation of it. Katie, thank you for writing beside me, reading my work, and inspiring me with your own.

I am grateful to all the writers whose work kept me company through this process, particularly my friend Aimee Seu, whose book of poems *Velvet Hounds* gave me the courage to write the essay 'Telling'.

Café Belle in Charlottesville, my sanctuary in new motherhood, is where much of *We All Come Home Alive* was written.

Thank you, for everything, to the family I came from and can't seem to stop writing about: my parents Mike and Nicki, and my brothers Max and John.

F, my star and my centre, thank you.

And thank you Luke, always. For knowing I'd write about our life and marrying me anyway. And the rest. You were it, you know: the best that could happen.

DISCOVER MORE FROM ANNA BEECHER

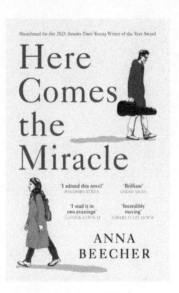

**Shortlisted for the 2021 *Sunday Times*
Young Writer of the Year Award**

It begins with a miracle: a baby born too small and too early,
but defiantly alive. This is Joe.

Then, two years later, Emily arrives. From the beginning,
the siblings' lives are entwined.

Snake back through time. In a patch of nettle-infested wilderness,
find Edward, seventeen years old, and falling in love with another
boy. In comes somebody else, Eleanor, with whom Edward starts
a family. They find themselves grandparents to Joe and Emily.

When Joe is diagnosed with cancer, the family are left waiting
for a miracle.

'*Here Comes the Miracle* may be a story about loss but it is also a
testimony to life, survival and the revitalising powers of memory'
IRISH TIMES

'I adored this novel' PANDORA SYKES